family finances

Making And Managing Money

by Joe McGee

Compiled from a *Faith For Families* seminar

Family Finances: Making and Managing Money
ISBN 978-0-9710450-5-7
Copyright © 2005 by Joe McGee
P. O. Box 61498
Tulsa, OK 74169-1498

Editor: Linda A. Schantz
Cover Design: Hampton Creative, Tulsa, OK

dedication

To Denise and the kids

for the invaluable lessons they have taught me

about the rewards of managing and increasing

every area of our lives.

A special thank you to my editor–Linda Schantz–

without whose belief in this project and sheer tenacity

this book would still be a stack of notes in my file cabinet.

table of contents

foreword

Joe McGee first came to our church in June of 1992, where he presented his *Faith For The Family Seminar.* Three things happened that summer which continue to this day. First, I met a man of integrity who is committed to serving our Lord and Savior. Second, I became acquainted with a man who is not only deeply devoted to his own wife and six children, but is wholeheartedly committed to strengthening the families of this generation and the generation to come. Third, I met a man in that summer whom I now call my friend.

Joe is a gifted communicator who, with his humor and simplicity, can make a difficult subject easy to understand and applicable to real life. That is what he does in this book. *Family Finances* is thorough and uncomplicated to read and use. I appreciate how he incorporates scriptural principles to help the reader become a better steward of God's resources.

One of the things I have discovered in my pastoral ministry is that many Christians do not understand the definition of "stewardship." Most people think that stewardship is only about money. They have never understood that Biblical stewardship includes *everything* that God has given them. In this book, Joe makes sense out of Biblical stewardship. He challenges us to rethink our attitudes about prosperity, money and our possessions.

I am excited to recommend this book to those people who want to expand their understanding of the Biblical approach to finances and true prosperity. *Family Finances* doesn't just inform and inspire, but it will be a useful tool that readers will want to refer to time and time again as they make financial decisions.

What I love about Joe is the fact that he not only has common-sense insights on the subject of family finances, but he lives those principles and Biblical truths in his own life. I guess that's why I have had Joe come back to our church every year since 1992 to help our families learn to live in God's very best.

> Dr. J. Michael Burns
> Senior Pastor
> Word of Victory Outreach Center
> Canton, Texas

how to use this manual
by Joe McGee

First, let me tell you that *I am not a financial expert.* I am not a financial advisor. I have a daughter who is an accountant, but I'm not an accountant. I'm just a husband and a father. I am a business owner, but in this manual, I'm just going to share what I've learned as somebody with some everyday common sense right out of the Word of God.

This handbook is designed to be used primarily as a springboard for you to gain more knowledge and insight so you can manage your own family's finances. *This manual is not the only book with financial information you'll ever need.*

There are some great books at your local bookstore about finances. Some are written from a Christian perspective and some are written by secular authors. At the end of this book, I'll give you a list of some resources that you can take advantage of to get more detailed direction in the things we're going to be covering. This book is simply a map to help you get headed in the right direction.

This manual is a collection of what I hope will be helpful information, charts, statistics, and forms for you to use to begin to get your financial life in order. I've included tons of scriptures, because I believe serving God and obeying His Word are the keys to financial well being.

Deuteronomy 8:18 tells us that it is the Lord who gives us the power to get wealth so that we might establish His covenant on the earth. If we take steps to bring our finances in line with the Word of God and the principles of His wisdom, God will bless us and prosper us in order to lead others to Him.

> *Any enterprise is built by wise planning, becomes strong through common sense, and profits wonderfully by keeping abreast of the facts.*
> *Proverbs 24:3-4 TLB*

It is my desire that this book will help you to learn how to walk responsibly in the area of finances concerning your family and that it will also take you to a new level of financial freedom and prosperity so you can be a blessing to others. By committing yourself to wise planning, by searching out the common sense that comes from God's Word, and by keeping abreast of the facts, your family can not only survive in this world's economy—it can thrive!

May God richly bless you and your family as you seek to follow Him.

family finances

An Overview

But if anyone does not provide for his own, and especially for those of his household, he has denied the faith and is worse than an unbeliever.
I Timothy 5:8 NKJV

That's a powerful scripture that can put some conviction on you. If you live in a house or an apartment, whether you have a single-parent household, or a two-parent household, whether you have one kid, two kids, six kids, or no children, you know it costs money to run a household today. My wife and I have six kids, and we have a household full of consumers. It takes a lot of money for us to live.

I have been teaching on the family for more than twenty years now, and I've covered some 384 subjects over that time. The one area that seems to cause people the most heartache and to bring up the most difficult questions is the area of finances and trying to provide for a family.

The cost of living keeps going up. Inflation is on the rise. The job market seems to be unsteady. In the Last Days, the Bible talks about perilous times coming. We know Jesus is coming back and we're excited about being a part of the End-Time harvest of souls, but Christians are crying out, "What about my home?" and "How am I going to take care of my family?"

God hasn't left us without answers. I believe He has provided us everything we need to take care of our families, but we're going to have to get into His Word to find out how to receive it.

In this book, we're going to be taking an in-depth look into **FAMILY FINANCES.** I've broken this subject down into four main areas. These are the things I cover when I'm talking to my own children about their finances. These are the things I would tell you if I was counseling with you personally.

The first area we need to look at is our attitudes, beliefs and behavior. I'm going to call the first section **BLESSED OR BROKE.** You're either blessed or you're broke. To be broke means you're insolvent, you're bankrupt, or simply, that your debts outweigh your assets. Unfortunately more people seem to be on that side of the river in these days than ever before.

What we want to do is look at our attitudes and beliefs about money, because they affect our behavior. If we want to get out of the "broke" category, what are we going to need?

We're going to need a new way of thinking.

> *And be not conformed to this world: but be ye transformed by the renewing of your mind, that ye may prove what is that good, and acceptable, and perfect, will of God.*
>
> *Romans 12:2*

Even though I'm born again and Spirit filled, I still have old thoughts. When I got born again, my spirit became a new creature in Christ. Old things passed away and all things were made new (I Corinthians 5:17), but my soul—or my mind, and my way of thinking—became my responsibility. God said, "I'm going to save your spirit, Joe, but your soul is your responsibility. That's why I've given you My Word. You do natural things, and I do supernatural things."

That's a common theme that runs through the Word of God. We do natural things, and God does supernatural things. We walk around the walls of Jericho. God knocks them down. We lay hands on the sick. He does the healing. We preach the Gospel. He does the saving.

Man's part when God placed him here was to take dominion over things. God told Adam in the Garden of Eden, "I want you to take dominion over the earth. I want you to subdue it. I want you to be fruitful and multiply." Everything God asked Adam to do was natural. If we'll do the natural, He'll do the supernatural.

The way we accelerate the supernatural in our lives is to make sure that we're doing the natural. That means we must be obedient to the Word of God. As we go through the first section of this book, we're going to find out what our part is. What are we supposed to be doing in order for God to do the supernatural on our behalf?

We need to examine our attitudes, beliefs and behavior when it comes to finances, because poverty originates in our souls—not in our bank accounts. How many times have we heard about someone who won the lottery or received a large sum of money in an inheritance, and they lost all of it, got divorced, and went bankrupt within a short time after that?

Great amounts of money won't deliver us if we don't have prosperity in our souls. To have prosperous souls we have to renew our minds and get rid of our old thoughts. We have to realize that our current financial condition is a result of our current financial thinking.

> *As a man thinks in his heart, so is he....*
>
> *Proverbs 23:7*

If we're going to become better off financially than we currently are, we're going to have to change our way of thinking. We have what we have now, because that's the way we think.

> *Beloved, I wish above all things that thou mayest prosper and be in health, even as thy soul prospereth.*
>
> *III John 2*

Everybody loves to quote this scripture because it means that God wants us to prosper. But it says that prosperity starts in our souls. We need to know the difference between God's way of thinking and the world's way of thinking when it comes to money, and we're going to have to change our thinking to line up with the Word of God.

The second section of this book is going to be devoted to conducting a **FINANCIAL HOUSE CLEANING.** Once we get our attitudes lined up with the Word of God, we've got to do something natural to get God to move supernaturally on our behalf. *We have to put our financial lives in order, because order precedes increase.*

I've spoken to so many people who need help with their finances and I've asked them, "How much do you owe?"

"We don't know," they tell me. "We're just in trouble."

I'll ask, "Where are your bank statements?" and "How much money do you have?"

They'll say, "Some of our statements are on the kitchen table, and some are in the bedroom. Some are in the den. They're scattered all over the house."

Friends, the first thing we need to do—before God can do His part—is establish some type of financial order. This is a very natural process, but it has major spiritual consequences.

The Word tells us that destruction comes from a lack of knowledge, and where there is no vision—that is, no plan—we will surely perish (Hosea 4:6, Proverbs 29:18).

We're going to have to find our starting point. Then we're going to have to create a spending plan. We have to start spending less and saving more. We're going to have to learn to manage the credit we've got. We're going to have to learn how to get out of debt. And we're going to have to have some kind of system to monitor our progress.

Before God can take us somewhere, we've got to find out where we are.

In the third section, we're going to look at **CHANNELS OF INCOME.** Once we get our attitudes right and all of our stuff is together, we have to be in the process of changing things. We'll be looking at gifts, callings, vocations and work. If we don't work, we don't eat.

We need two things to make it in life: work and faith. The Bible says without faith, we can't please God (Hebrews 11:6). It also says that faith without works is dead (James 2:20). So we need jobs and we need to trust in God.

We need to recognize that we live in two different economies. We live in the economy of Heaven, which involves faith. Faith is the currency of Heaven's economy. If we don't have faith, we can't please God. But we also live on this planet. Cash is the currency of the economy here. We get cash for two things here. We get paid for what we know, and for what we do. If we're going to prosper so that we can provide for our families, we're going to have to find something—a gift, or a tool—that we can use to generate income.

> *Even while we were still there with you we gave you this rule: "He who does not work shall not eat."*
>
> *II Thessalonians 3:10 TLB*

We need to find out what our gifts are. We need to find out what we're called to do. What makes us valuable, and what are we going to do that somebody is going to pay us money for?

If we want to get paid more, we've got to do something to make ourselves more valuable. That's how we're going to provide for our families and prosper.

The fourth and final area we're going to look at in this book is **THE POWER TO GET WEALTH—SOWING AND REAPING.** When the children of Israel were in the land of Egypt, it was *the land of never enough.*

When God brought them out of Israel into the wilderness, it was *the land of just enough.* Manna came every day except for the sabbath. Their clothes never wore out. Their shoes lasted for forty years. Nobody bothered the Israelites much in the wilderness.

But once they crossed the Jordan River into the land of Canaan, the Bible says the manna stopped. There was no manna there, because they were in *the land of seedtime and harvest—the land of sowing and reaping.* They were able to provide for themselves. They were able to grow crops and do things on their own. So they went from the land of not enough, into the land of just enough, but *God's ultimate purpose was for them to go into the land of more than enough.*

God's purpose for our families is not just for them to survive. That's not Biblical. He wants us to thrive. We have to thrive because inflation alone is eating up 3% to 5% of our money every year. We've got to find a way of making more money than we're currently making just to keep up with inflation.

But that's not the only reason we need to thrive. The Bible says that a good man leaves an inheritance to his family (Proverbs 13:22). So not only do we need enough to survive on today, we've got to leave an inheritance behind us for our children and for their children.

How are we going to do that?

We're going to have to learn how money makes money. We're going to have to study God's principles of increase—tithing and giving, and sowing and reaping. The blessings of God follow obedience to the laws of God. I'm going to have to find out what those laws are.

There are a lot of warnings and a lot of commandments about money in the Bible and we're going to try to cover as many of them as possible. Then we'll know how to tap into the things God has provided for us.

There have been so many things taught in churches about money. Some of it is good, and some of it's not good. Some Christians talk about money like God is in the business of giving everyone "get-rich-quick" schemes. But the Bible says, if we get money fast, we'll lose it fast. We want enduring riches. We want the things that God wants to give us, but in order to receive them, we've got to get some knowledge, and we have to be obedient to what His Word tells us to do.

There is more said in the New Testament about money than there is about Heaven and Hell combined. Money is not just natural. It's a very spiritual issue.

Did you know that the word *believe* is in the Bible 272 times?

That's a lot.

The word *praise* is in the Bible 371 times.

The word *love* is in the Bible 714 times. God is love. Love is so important. Love is the fruit we've got to have. Even faith works by love.

But did you know the word *give* is in the Bible 2,162 times?!

Giving and money are real heart issues. The Bible is full of principles that will enable us to be financially successful, but we're going to have to follow them.

> *The whole Bible was given to us by inspiration from God and is useful to teach us what is true and to make us realize what is wrong in our lives; it straightens us out and helps us do what is right. It is God's way of making us well prepared at every point, fully equipped to do good to everyone.*
> *II Timothy 3:16-17 TLB*

We're going to go to the Word and find out what God said about money. We can see from the statistics in the first section of this book that there's a hole in our thinking on this planet concerning money.

The devil is a thief. He comes to steal, to kill and to destroy. The world's system doesn't operate like God's. It hoards up. It's fearful. It's afraid. But God expects the righteous to be as bold as a lion. We're to be the salt and the light of the earth. We're to be the givers—the ones who are blessed. God told Abraham, I want to bless you so I can make you a blessing (Genesis 12:2, 3).

So let's look now at how we're going to get those channels of income to flow through us to this lost and dying world.

$ection 1

blessed
or broke?

Attitudes, Beliefs
And Behavior

blessed
or broke?

ATTITUDES, BELIEFS AND BEHAVIOR

WHAT WE NEED:

A new way of thinking about finances

WHY WE NEED IT:

Poverty is a curse. It's a condition of the soul, not of the pocketbook.

HOW DO WE CHANGE OUR THINKING?

We must renew our minds with the Word of God.

In this section, we'll look at what has shaped our beliefs about money, how our attitudes affect our current financial condition, and how we can get motivated to change our behavior today.

> *Beloved, I wish above all things that thou mayest prosper and be in health even as thy soul prospers.*
>
> *III John 2*

WEALTH CONSCIOUSNESS

Years ago, I read a wonderful book called *Wealth Happens One Day At A Time,* by Brooke Stephens (New York, NY: HarperCollins, 1999). In it, Stephens makes a very important point about what she calls our "wealth consciousness." Her research (which should come as no surprise) showed that our parents and the influential people in our lives when we were growing up greatly define what we come to believe as adults about our own abilities to prosper.

In other words, if we grew up believing that we were undeserving or unable to have any of the material things that would make our lives easier or more enjoyable, then no matter how hard we work, or how quickly we accomplish our financial goals, our attitudes and underlying beliefs about ourselves will eventually destroy them.

Our own personal "wealth consciousness" is how we have come to think, feel and act about money. Our thought patterns and beliefs clearly affect all the choices we make about money.

Many of us were continually told by our parents, "Money doesn't grow on trees," or "We can't afford that." Those negative messages have been deeply ingrained in us from childhood.

Even though most of us may earn more money and be better educated than our parents, their old, wrong thinking runs through our souls. Yet our attitude toward money is the most important factor in improving our financial future.

The only way to break down a lifetime of wrong financial concepts and habits is to develop some better ones. We can only do that by renewing our minds with the Word of God (Romans 12:2).

REAL MEN ACCEPT RESPONSIBILITY

> *But if anyone does not provide for his own, and especially for those of his household, he has denied the faith and is worse than an unbeliever.*
> *I Timothy 5:8 NKJV*

According to this scripture, God has put the responsibility to provide for our families on us. If God has given us this responsibility, then there must be a way for us to do it. What we need to do is find out how to do it from the Word of God.

The Bible is the greatest book on financial security that's ever been written. It's full of principles and precepts on how to act and how to live. It's also full of examples that demonstrate how God gives great rewards to those who are willing to take responsibility.

The first Adam did not take responsibility in any of the things God gave him to do. He had clear instructions, but Adam didn't do what was required of him.

He was to keep and cultivate the Garden of Eden and protect his family, but he didn't do it. Adam got fired from his job because he was disobedient and he rejected his responsibility.

Jesus—the Second Adam—took all the responsibility His Father gave Him. He was sent to redeem the lost through His death on the cross. He accomplished His work and said, "It is finished." Because He accepted His responsibility, today Jesus is seated at the right hand of the Father with a name that is above every name!

ESAU AND JACOB

There's another great story about taking responsibility in the Bible. In the story of Jacob and Esau, we find that Esau did not value what God valued.

In the Old Testament, it was the right of the firstborn son in every family to receive the double blessing. The reason for this was because the oldest son was supposed to be the future head of the tribe. Esau, as the firstborn son, would have had advantages and privileges his brothers would never have gotten.

As the oldest son, Esau was supposed to get his share like everybody else in the family when Isaac died, but Esau was also supposed to get a second part of the inheritance (a double portion), which would have enabled him to provide food, clothing, shelter and whatever else was necessary to care for his mother, his unmarried sisters, the orphans, the widows and the unemployed of his tribe.

But Esau said, "I don't want to be responsible for anybody other than myself. I only want my portion. I don't want the second portion. I don't want to take care of Mom, my sisters, and the orphans. I don't care anything about them."

So Esau sold his birthright to his brother Jacob for a bowl of beans one day.

Some people say, "Yeah, but, Jacob was a liar and a cheat."

You know he was, but God said this, "Jacob have I loved. Esau have I hated."

How could the Lord hate a child that hadn't even been born yet?

The answer is that God saw the future. He saw the choices Esau was going to make and how he didn't value what God had provided (Hebrews 12:16). Esau despised his birthright (Genesis 25:34).

Jacob, on the other hand, wanted the blessings *and* he wanted the responsibility. He wanted to be able to take care of people other than his own thumb-sucking self. Jacob wanted the responsibility of providing for others.

So in effect, God was saying, "I don't like people who go through life not wanting to be responsible for others."

Responsibility is an honor. God loves people who want to be responsible for other people. He'll provide for us. He'll give us more, if we're willing to become responsible. Taking responsibility is a great way of increasing our income. Taking responsibility includes understanding the part we have to play in our economic success.

THE TWO ECONOMIES

As believers, we function in two different economies. We function in God's economy, but we also function in the world's economy. We have responsibilities in each, if we want to have success.

THE SOURCE OF OUR FINANCIAL SECURITY

In God's economy, the source of our financial security is God. He owns everything and He provides. Jesus doesn't want us worrying about our finances.

> *Then Jesus said to his disciples: "Therefore I tell you, do not worry about your life, what you will eat; or about your body, what you will wear. Who of you by worrying can add a single hour to his life?*
>
> *Luke 12:22, 25 NIV*

> *Consider how the lilies grow. They do not labor or spin. Yet I tell you, not even Solomon in all his splendor was dressed like one of these. If that is how God clothes the grass of the field, which is here today, and tomorrow is thrown into the fire, how much more will he clothe you, O you of little faith! And do not set your heart on what you will eat or drink; do not worry about it. For the pagan world runs after all such things, and your Father knows that you need them. But seek his kingdom, and these things will be given to you as well.*
>
> *Luke 12:27-31 NIV*

> *I was young and now I am old, yet I have never seen the righteous forsaken or their children begging bread.*
>
> *Psalm 37:25 NIV*

> *But my God shall supply all your need according to his riches in glory by Christ Jesus.*
>
> *Philippians 4:19*

> *Now unto him that is able to do exceeding abundantly above all that we ask or think, according to the power that worketh in us...*
>
> *Ephesians 3:20*

In the world's economy, our source of financial security comes from our vocation or job, from our insurance, our stocks and bonds, from the family inheritance and our talents. In the world's economy, to be financially secure, we've got to use some natural tools, but in God's economy we've got to use some spiritual tools to prosper.

THE KEYS TO SUCCESS IN GOD'S ECONOMY

In God's economy there are two keys to success—obedience and faith.

1. **Obedience**

   We've got to be obedient to God to have success in His economy.

   If they obey and serve him, they shall spend their days in prosperity, and their years in pleasures.

   Job 36:11

   If ye be willing and obedient, ye shall eat the good of the land.

   Isaiah 1:19

2. **Faith**

   We also have to have faith. Faith is the currency of God's economy. Without faith, we can't please God. Whatever is not of faith is sin. Sin's got death attached to it and it will kill us spiritually, mentally, physically and financially. We've got to have faith.

   Where does faith come from?

   It comes from God's Word.

   So then faith cometh by hearing, and hearing by the word of God.

   Romans 10:17

   But without faith it is impossible to please him: for he that cometh to God must believe that he is, and that he is a rewarder of them that diligently seek him.

   Hebrews 11:6

   Now the just shall live by faith: but if any man draw back, my soul shall have no pleasure in him.

   Hebrews 10:38

In God's economy the keys to success are obedience and faith, but in order to have success here on earth, we're going to have to work and do some natural things.

THE KEYS TO SUCCESS IN THE WORLD'S ECONOMY

There are three keys to financial success in the world's economy.

1. Hard Work

In this world, if we want to have plenty, we have to work.

And that ye study to be quiet, and to do your own business, and to work with your own hands, as we commanded you; That ye may walk honestly toward them that are without, and that ye may have lack of nothing.

I Thessalonians 4:11-12

Now here is a command dear brothers, given in the name of our Lord Jesus Christ by his authority: Stay away from any Christian who spends his days in laziness and does not follow the ideal of hard work we set up for you. For you well know that you ought to follow our example: you never saw us loafing; we never accepted food from anyone without buying it; we worked hard day and night for the money we needed to live on, in order that we would not be a burden to any of you. It wasn't that we didn't have the right to ask you to feed us, but we wanted to show you firsthand how you should work for your living. Even while we were still with you, we gave you this rule; "He who does not work shall not eat." Yet we hear that some of you are living in laziness, refusing to work, wasting your time in gossiping. In the name of the Lord Jesus Christ we appeal to such people—we command them—to quiet down, get to work, and earn their own living.

II Thessalonians 3:6-12 TLB

2. Knowledge

In the world's economy, we're also going to have to increase our abilities. To do that, we need knowledge.

My people are destroyed for lack of knowledge...

Hosea 4:6

I wisdom dwell with prudence, and find out knowledge of witty inventions.

Proverbs 8:12

Through wisdom is a house built, and by understanding is it established; By knowledge the rooms are filled with all precious and pleasant riches.

Proverbs 24:3-4 NKJV

If we go back and read about the greatest men of miracles in the Old Testament, we'll find that those men just happen to be the most educated men of the Old Testament, as well. The greatest miracle man of the New Testament—Paul—also happened to be the most educated man of the New Testament. That's not a coincidence.

Look at the story of Joseph for an example. Joseph, the boy with the coat of many colors, whose brothers hated him for his dreams and visions, was to feed the known world in a time of famine. That was his destiny in life. But he couldn't do it from Israel, because the bread factory was going to be in Egypt. So he had to get to Egypt.

It wasn't a great trip. His brothers sold him as a slave. He was working in Potiphar's house, but look what happened. He learned a lot of natural things, like how much food an Egyptian ate, how much money it took to run an Egyptian household, how much grain an Egyptian camel consumed, etc. In other words, Joseph learned firsthand how much it took to run an Egyptian household.

Joseph learned to deal with irate and cranky people in a time of famine.

How did he learn that?

He learned it working in prison. Then when God supernaturally promoted Joseph, he was ready in the natural to handle it.

So if we want to be promoted in this world's economy, we're going to have to learn some natural things. God uses our natural abilities. Read the parable in Matthew 25. Our natural abilities are critical to success in this world. We've got to increase and improve them through knowledge.

3. Visions And Plans

Visions and plans are the third part of success in a worldly economy. We've got to have a dream. We have to have a vision.

Where there is no vision, the people perish...

Proverbs 29:18

Commit to the LORD whatever you do, and your plans will succeed. In his heart a man plans his course, but the LORD determines his steps.

Proverbs 16:3, 9 NIV

It's Biblical to have a plan. God had a plan. He planned out the earth. In Psalm 139:16, God says all the days of our lives were written in Heaven before we were ever born. God planned out our lives and our future, and He wants us to follow His plan.

MEDIUM OF EXCHANGE

The medium of exchange in God's economy is faith, and the medium of exchange in the world is currency—cold, hard cash. So we'd better know how to get both of them. The two work side by side.

> Here mortal men receive tithes, but there he receives them, of whom it is witnessed that he lives.
>
> Hebrews 7:8 NKJV

Men get our currency, and God gets our faith. Hebrews 7:8 tells us that when we pay our tithes, we're working both economies at the same time.

> After Jesus and his disciples arrived in Capernaum, the collectors of the two-drachma tax came to Peter and asked, "Doesn't your teacher pay the temple tax?" "Yes, he does," he replied. When Peter came into the house, Jesus was the first to speak. "What do you think, Simon?" he asked. "From whom do the kings of the earth collect duty and taxes—from their own sons or from others?" "From others," Peter answered. "Then the sons are exempt," Jesus said to him. "But so that we may not offend them, go to the lake and throw out your line. Take the first fish you catch; open its mouth and you will find a four-drachma coin. Take it and give it to them for my tax and yours."
>
> Matthew 17:24-27 NIV

Jesus recognized that He functioned in two economies. He understood this principle very well.

THE UNJUST STEWARD—LESSONS FROM A SHREWD ACCOUNTANT

> Jesus told his disciples: "There was a rich man whose manager was accused of wasting his possessions. So he called him in and asked him, 'What is this I hear about you? Give an account of your management, because you cannot be manager any longer.' "The manager said to himself, 'What shall I do now? My master is taking away my job. I'm not strong enough to dig, and I'm ashamed to beg—I know what I'll do so that, when I lose my job here, people will welcome me into their houses.' "So he called in each one of his master's debtors. He asked the first, 'How much do you owe my master?' "'Eight hundred gallons of olive oil,' he replied. "The manager told him, 'Take your bill, sit down quickly, and make it four hundred.' "Then he asked the second, 'And how much do you owe?' "'A thousand bushels of wheat,' he replied. "He told him, 'Take your bill and make it eight hundred.' "The master commended the dishonest manager because he had acted shrewdly. For the people of this world are more shrewd in dealing with their own kind than are the people of the light. I tell you, use

worldly wealth to gain friends for yourselves, so that when it is gone, you will be welcomed into eternal dwellings. "Whoever can be trusted with very little can also be trusted with much, and whoever is dishonest with very little will also be dishonest with much. So if you have not been trustworthy in handling worldly wealth, who will trust you with true riches? And if you have not been trustworthy with someone else's property, who will give you property of your own? "No servant can serve two masters. Either he will hate the one and love the other, or he will be devoted to the one and despise the other. You cannot serve both God and Money." The Pharisees, who loved money, heard all this and were sneering at Jesus. He said to them, "You are the ones who justify yourselves in the eyes of men, but God knows your hearts. What is highly valued among men is detestable in God's sight.

Luke 16:1-15 NIV

There's a great saying we need to commit to memory:

> ***Money and God—God and money***
> ***One we serve—The other serves us***

We have to keep those two straight! Money is not a god. It has no emotion— no personality. Within itself, it has no evil. Money is not out to get us. What it is and what it becomes is what we make it. If we get our eyes off God and get them on our money, then our attitudes are going to change, and the heart issue is going to come into play.

There are five lessons we can learn from the accountant in Luke 16.

1. **We can learn some things by looking at why the shrewd accountant was commended.** He wasn't commended for lying or for stealing. So what did his master commend him for?

   - He was commended for doing well for himself. He had enough sense to take care of himself.

   - He was commended for knowing how to improve his present opportunity.

   - He was commended for knowing how to provide for a future need.

2. **Jesus said that the people of this world are wiser than the children of light.** Why is that?

   - Though Christians know there's another world coming, we don't prepare for it. We talk about Heaven, but we don't get ready for it.

- Though we're told we will shortly be turned out of our stewardship, we live and act like we're going to be here forever.

- Men of this world use their natural wisdom to manage their money not just for today, but so they will have the benefit of it later in life. They put their money out to interest, buy land with it and invest in stocks and bonds.

- Believers don't make good use of their possessions in this world to provide for a comfortable life here or for a good reception in the life to come. We're supposed to use our money to provide for our families, to make sure our bills are paid, to be a blessing to people and to lay up treasures in Heaven.

3. **Jesus says if we're faithful in the least, we will be faithful also in much.** In other words, he who serves God and does good things with his money will serve God with the more noble and valuable riches of wisdom, grace, spiritual gifts and the souls of men.

    The measuring stick God uses for our souls on this planet is how we handle money. The Bible says where a man's heart is, his treasure is.

    Do you want to know how a man will handle spiritual things?

    Look at his checkbook.

4. **If we bury one talent of the world's wealth, we'll never improve the five talents of spiritual riches.** God withholds His grace from covetous, worldly people more than we realize.

5. **We need to pay our debts.** If we aren't faithful with other people's money, why should we be trusted with money of our own?

YOU CAN LOVE GOD AND STILL DIE BROKE

Second Kings 4:1 talks about a widow whose husband had recently died. It was said of her husband that he feared and served God, but yet, he still died broke. He had knowledge of God, but he evidently had no knowledge of money.

The Bible says, *"A good man leaves an inheritance for his children's children...."* (Proverbs 13:22). By that standard, this man was not a good man. Yes, he was a godly man, in that he feared God, but Elisha could have told the woman, "Your husband worked for me, but he had no sense about money. He left you so far in debt that your sons are going to be slaves the rest of their lives."

Can you imagine getting to Heaven and everybody saying, "Well, I'm glad you made it, but you left your wife and kids in a mess on the earth!"? Friends, that's not right! That's not what God wants for His children.

Not only do we need to learn how to take care of our families financially now, we also need to put back money for them in the future. God doesn't want you to be barely getting by, leaving nothing for your kids. He wants you to have abundant life. He wants you to have above and beyond—to be the head and not the tail.

So why is it that, as Christians, sometimes we're struggling just to reach average?

Let's take a look at what "average" is in America.

AVERAGE FAMILY INCOME AND EXPENDITURES

Data taken from The U.S. Census Bureau 2000-2003 Consumer Expenditure Survey

AVERAGE U.S. HOUSEHOLD GROSS INCOME (2003) $51,128

AVERAGE HOUSEHOLD EXPENDITURES *EXCLUDING TAXES* (2003) $40,817

HOUSEHOLD EXPENDITURE	% OF EXPENSES	AVG/YR	AVG/MO
Housing	32.9%	$13,432	$1,119
Includes Utilities, Public Services 6.9%			
Includes Furnishings, Equipment 3.7%			
Transportation	19.1%	$7,781	$648
Personal Insurance/Pensions	9.9%	$4,055	$338
Food At Home	7.7%	$3,129	$261
Healthcare	5.9%	$2,416	$201
Food Away From Home	5.4%	$2,211	$184
Entertainment	5.0%	$2,060	$172
Apparel Products And Services	4.0%	$1,640	$137
Education	1.9%	$783	$65
Alcoholic Beverages	1.0%	$391	$33
Tobacco Products	0.7%	$290	$24
Cash Contributions	3.4%	$1,370	$114
Other	3.1%	$1,259	$104

TOTAL U.S. FAMILY EXPENDITURES 100% $40,817   *$3,401
    Excluding Income Taxes

AVERAGE U.S. FAMILY GROSS INCOME $51,128   *$4,261
    *Rounded to the nearest whole amount

THE COST OF CHILDREN

Data taken from The USDA Center for Nutrition Policy and Promotion, "Expenditures on Children by Families Year 2004 Annual Report"

The median income for families with children $53,692

Cost to raise one child to age 18 (by a middle-income family) $184,320
Families with three or more children spend an average of 23% less per child.

Acquisition Costs (Childbirth And Pre-Natal Care)

Average cost of an uncomplicated normal delivery $7,090

Average Caesarean delivery costs $11,450

Child Care

Average annual child-care costs for a middle-class three- to five-year old $1,680
Fully 56% of American families with children use paid child care.

Food

Average annual cost to feed one middle-class child under age two $1,170

Average annual food cost for a middle-class 15-year old $2,270

Transportation

Average annual additional transportation costs for a middle-class child $1,950
Parents with teenagers spend over 70% more than families with infants.

Health Care

The average cost of keeping a middle-class child healthy to age 18 $13,830

Clothing

Average cost of keeping an only child properly dressed to age 18 $9,930
According to the Bureau of Labor Statistics, families spend nearly 18% more to clothe girls than boys.

Primary And Secondary Education

Average costs for public education of a child to age 18 $12,420
Fully 89% of all school age children in the U.S. attend public school. Public education costs American society more than $290 billion per year.

Personal Care Items, Entertainment Expenses and Reading Materials

Average costs for personal care and entertainment items for a child to 18 $19,980

College (The Largest Expense For Children After Age 17)

The College Board's estimated average annual tuition and fees in 2000-2001 were:

Annual tuition at a four-year public college	$3,420
Annual tuition at a four-year private college	$13,688
Annual room and board at a public college	$4,705
Annual room and board at a private college	$5,447
Annual tuition at a two-year public college	$1,655
Annual tuition at a two-year private college	$8,210

Note: A 1996 survey found that 47% of parents in their fifties support children over 21 years of age.
(Source: Phoenix Home Life Mutual Insurance Company)

WHAT DO ALL THESE EXPENSES COME TO?

The USDA Center for Nutrition Policy and Promotion calculates that a typical middle-class, husband-wife family will spend a total of $184,320 to raise an only child from birth to age 18!

I've got six kids. Although families with more than three children spend about 23% less per child, that still means I'm going to need almost $1 million just to raise my kids to age 18 and get them out of the house! That doesn't include higher education, or if they stay in my home past age 18, 20, or 22, until they get out of college or get married.

MORE FACTS AND FIGURES

- 75.2% of all American families carry some kind of debt.

- 17.8% of all American families with children under 18 live in poverty.

- 55.6% of all American children under six who are living in a household with a female head (no husband present) live in poverty. *(That's five times the rate of the counterparts in married-couple families.)*

- 24.3% of all families in America are single-parent families.

- Only 26% of all families in America are comprised of a father, a mother and children under the age of 18, compared to 45% in 1972.

- Single adults with no kids make up 32% of all households in America.

- 25% of all families in America either directly or indirectly own stock.

- The majority of all sophomores plan to go to college right after high school. *(They have no idea how they're going to pay for it.)*

- 69% of all mothers with children under the age of six are employed outside the home. *(Today, the two-earner family is the norm, not the exception.)*

- Three-fourths of all school-aged children have working mothers.

- Not only are 75% of America's households in debt, but 55% owe more than they own in financial assets. (Incidentally, one out of two marriages ends in divorce. Sixty percent of divorcées cite financial pressure as a major cause of their divorce.)

- 85% of all Americans are one paycheck away from financial disaster.

- The majority of all Americans will retire with less than $10,000 in annual income. *(That's poverty! In the last decade, 60,000 U.S. companies did away with their pension plans.)*

- 85% of Americans 65 and older have less than $250 in savings. *(Two companies in America employ more senior citizens than anyone else: Wal-Mart and McDonald's.)*

- 87% of all Americans claim to be evangelical Christians who know God.

That means most people can honestly say, "We know God, but we're retiring broke. We're not leaving anything behind for our children but debts."

Americans have missed something somewhere! We need to find out what that is and get back on track.

THE GOVERNMENT TRACKS PEOPLE

The U.S. Department of Health, Education and Welfare tracked people in the United States from age 20 to 65 and found:

By age 65, for every 100 people tracked:

36 were dead
54 were living on government or family support
5 were still working because they had to
4 were well off
1 was actually wealthy

Did you get that?

Only five out of every one hundred people at retirement age were financially well off. Over half were living off of government support or living with their relatives because they couldn't afford to live on their own. Five more were working because they had to.

We've got a bad situation in this country that we're going to have to turn around. Good people—even godly people—do not understand how to manage their money well enough to provide for themselves in retirement, let alone how to leave an inheritance for their children's children. That's not God's plan.

FINANCIAL WARNINGS

The only way we're going to learn to prosper is to dig into the Bible and find out what God has to say about money. First let's take a look at the financial warnings. There are ten warnings concerning money found in the Word.

1. Don't love money. Love God.

> *For the love of money is a root of all kinds of evil. Some people, eager for money, have wandered from the faith and pierced themselves with many griefs.*
> *I Timothy 6:10 NIV*

If we make money a god and don't put it in the right perspective, we'll never have any. That's not God's will for us or our families.

2. Don't become a slave to money.

> *No one can serve two masters. Either he will hate the one and love the other, or he will be devoted to the one and despise the other. You cannot serve both God and Money.*
> *Matthew 6:24 NIV*

Money is simply a tool. We're supposed to use it to help us accomplish the things God wants us to do.

3. Wealth is deceitful and can choke the Word in your life.

> *Still others, like seed sown among thorns, hear the word; but the worries of this life, the deceitfulness of wealth and the desires for other things come in and choke the word, making it unfruitful.*
> *Mark 4:18-19 NIV*

4. It is hard for rich people to enter the kingdom of Heaven.

Then Jesus said to his disciples, "I tell you the truth, it is hard for a rich man to enter the kingdom of heaven. Again I tell you, it is easier for a camel to go through the eye of a needle than for a rich man to enter the kingdom of God."

Matthew 19:23-24 NIV

He didn't say it was impossible, He just said it was hard. *(See the next two warnings.)*

5. Never trust in wealth.

"Here now is the man who did not make God his stronghold but trusted in his great wealth and grew strong by destroying others!" But I am like an olive tree flourishing in the house of God; I trust in God's unfailing love for ever and ever.

Psalm 52:7-8 NIV

Whoever trusts in his riches will fall, but the righteous will thrive like a green leaf.

Proverbs 11:28 NIV

Command those who are rich in this present world not to be arrogant nor to put their hope in wealth, which is so uncertain, but to put their hope in God, who richly provides us with everything for our enjoyment.

I Timothy 6:17 NIV

6. Never set your heart on your riches.

Do not trust in extortion or take pride in stolen goods; though your riches increase, do not set your heart on them. One thing God has spoken, two things have I heard: that you, O God, are strong, and that you, O Lord, are loving. Surely you will reward each person according to what he has done.

Psalm 62:10-12 NIV

Cast but a glance at riches, and they are gone, for they will surely sprout wings and fly off to the sky like an eagle.

Proverbs 23:5 NIV

7. Wealth is worthless in the day of wrath.

Wealth is worthless in the day of wrath, but righteousness delivers from death.

Proverbs 11:4 NIV

You can't take it with you!

8. Beware of covetousness.

Then he said to them, "Watch out! Be on your guard against all kinds of greed; a man's life does not consist in the abundance of his possessions."

Luke 12:15 NIV

9. **To oppress the poor brings poverty.**

> *He who oppresses the poor to increase his wealth and he who gives gifts to the rich—both come to poverty.*
>
> > *Proverbs 22:16 NIV*

10. **He who gets rich quick will not go unpunished.**

> *A faithful man shall abound with blessings; but he who makes haste to be rich [at any cost] shall not be unpunished.*
>
> > *Proverbs 28:20 AMP*

Most of us have heard these warnings at some point in our lives. The bottom line is we don't have to worry about the snares of riches if our hearts are right.

GOD OWNS IT ALL

The breath we breathe, the life we live, the strength in our hands and in our bodies—whatever we possess in God—God gave it to us as a gift. We don't own anything! We're just managing it so we can pass it on to our children. Then they can manage it and pass it on to their children, and we can constantly be a blessing to our families, our churches, our communities and the world.

> *The earth is the LORD's, and the fulness thereof; the world, and they that dwell therein.*
>
> > *Psalm 24:1*

> *For every beast of the forest is mine, and the cattle upon a thousand hills. I know all the fowls of the mountains: and the wild beasts of the field are mine. If I were hungry, I would not tell thee: for the world is mine, and the fulness thereof.*
>
> > *Psalm 50:10-12*

WE ARE ONLY STEWARDS

> *For we brought nothing into this world, and it is certain we can carry nothing out.*
>
> > *I Timothy 6:7*

> *But whatever is good and perfect comes to us from God, the Creator of all light, and he shines forever without change or shadow.*
>
> > *James 1:17 TLB*

> *God has given each of you some special abilities; be sure to use them to help each other, passing on to others God's many kinds of blessings.*
>
> > *I Peter 4:10 TLB*

> *Moreover it is required in stewards, that a man be found faithful.*
>
> > *I Corinthians 4:2*

FINANCIAL COMMANDMENTS

Now to balance the warnings concerning money in God's Word, let's look at the financial commandments for just a moment. There are ten commandments God gives us concerning money in the Bible. I believe they're all self-explanatory.

1. **Pay God the first 10% of your increase. The tithe goes to your local church.**

   "Bring the whole tithe into the storehouse, that there may be food in my house. Test me in this," says the LORD Almighty, "and see if I will not throw open the floodgates of heaven and pour out so much blessing that you will not have room enough for it."

   Malachi 3:10 NIV

2. **Provide for your own family's financial needs.**

   But if any provide not for his own, and specially for those of his own house, he hath denied the faith, and is worse than an infidel.

   I Timothy 5:8

3. **Purchase a home for yourself and your family.**

   In the house of the wise are stores of choice food and oil, but a foolish man devours all he has.

   Proverbs 21:20 NIV

   The wise woman builds her house, but with her own hands the foolish one tears hers down.

   Proverbs 14:1 NIV

   Build ye houses, and dwell in them; and plant gardens, and eat the fruit of them....

   Jeremiah 29:5

   And every one that hath forsaken houses, or brethren, or sisters, or father, or mother, or wife, or children, or lands, for my name's sake, shall receive an hundredfold, and shall inherit everlasting life.

   Matthew 19:29

4. **Leave an inheritance for your children and grandchildren.**

   A good man leaveth an inheritance to his children's children: and the wealth of the sinner is laid up for the just.

   Proverbs 13:22

Now I am ready to visit you for the third time, and I will not be a burden to you, because what I want is not your possessions but you. After all, children should not have to save up for their parents, but parents for their children. So I will very gladly spend for you everything I have and expend myself as well....
                                                        II Corinthians 12:14-15 NIV

House and riches are the inheritance of fathers and a prudent wife is from the LORD.

                                                                    Proverbs 19:14

5. **Give to missions and other ministers.**

For it is written in the law of Moses, Thou shalt not muzzle the mouth of the ox that treadeth out the corn. Doth God take care for oxen? Or saith he it altogether for our sakes? For our sakes, no doubt, this is written: that he that ploweth should plow in hope; and that he that thresheth in hope should be partaker of his hope. If we have sown unto you spiritual things, is it a great thing if we shall reap your carnal things?
                                                            I Corinthians 9:9-11

6. **Pay your debts and your taxes.**

Let no debt remain outstanding, except the continuing debt to love one another, for he who loves his fellowman has fulfilled the law.
                                                                Romans 13:8 NIV

And Jesus answering said unto them, Render to Caesar the things that are Caesar's, and to God the things that are God's. And they marvelled at him.
                                                                    Mark 12:17

7. **Give to the poor and to organizations that aid the poor.**

He that hath pity upon the poor lendeth unto the LORD; and that which he hath given will he pay him again.
                                                                    Proverbs 19:17

He that giveth unto the poor shall not lack: but he that hideth his eyes shall have many a curse.
                                                                    Proverbs 28:27

A generous man will himself be blessed, for he shares his food with the poor.
                                                                Proverbs 22:9 NIV

8. **Give bountifully to every good work.**

But this I say, He which soweth sparingly shall reap also sparingly; and he which soweth bountifully shall reap also bountifully. Every man according as he purposeth in his heart, so let him give; not grudgingly, or of necessity: for God loveth a cheerful giver. And God is able to make all grace abound toward you; that ye, always having all sufficiency in all things, may abound to every good work:

II Corinthians 9:6-8

Now he who supplies seed to the sower and bread for food will also supply and increase your store of seed and will enlarge the harvest of your righteousness. You will be made rich in every way so that you can be generous on every occasion, and through us your generosity will result in thanksgiving to God. This service that you perform is not only supplying the needs of God's people but is also overflowing in many expressions of thanks to God.

II Corinthians 9:10-12 NIV

9. **Work with your own hands so you'll have something to share with those in need.**

He who has been stealing must steal no longer, but must work, doing something useful with his own hands, that he may have something to share with those in need.

Ephesians 4:28 NIV

"Behold, I am coming soon! My reward is with me, and I will give to everyone according to what he has done."

Revelation 22:12

10. **Lay up treasures in your Heavenly bank account.**

But store up for yourselves treasures in heaven, where moth and rust do not destroy, and where thieves do not break in and steal. For where your treasure is, there your heart will be also.

Matthew 6:20-21 NIV

POVERTY IS A CONDITION OF THE SOUL, NOT THE POCKETBOOK

Beloved, I wish above all things that thou mayest prosper and be in health, even as thy soul prospereth.

III John 2

This book of the law shall not depart out of thy mouth; but thou shalt meditate therein day and night, that thou mayest observe to do according to all that is written therein: for then thou shalt make thy way prosperous, and then thou shalt have good success.

Joshua 1:8

In both of these scriptures, ***God puts the responsibility of prosperity on us.*** If we'll meditate on God's Word and get our souls—our mind, will and emotions—right, then we'll be prosperous and we'll have good success.

Blessed is the man that walketh not in the counsel of the ungodly, nor standeth in the way of sinners, nor sitteth in the seat of the scornful. But his delight is in the law of the LORD; and in his law doth he meditate day and night. And he shall be like a tree planted by the rivers of water, that bringeth forth his fruit in his season; his leaf also shall not wither; and whatsoever he doeth shall prosper.

Psalm 1:1-3

(For the weapons of our warfare are not carnal, but mighty through God to the pulling down of strong holds;) Casting down imaginations, and every high thing that exalteth itself against the knowledge of God, and bringing into captivity every thought to the obedience of Christ...

II Corinthians 10:4-5

And be not conformed to this world: but be ye transformed by the renewing of your mind, that ye may prove what is that good, and acceptable, and perfect, will of God.

Romans 12:2

We have to get our thinking straight. If we're having problems with our money—if we're always in debt—if bill collectors are calling—our problem is not with cash. Our problem is the way we think.

Notice that we can tell ourselves what to think.

Finally, brethren, whatsoever things are true, whatsoever things are honest, whatsoever things are just, whatsoever things are pure, whatsoever things are lovely, whatsoever things are of good report; if there be any virtue, and if there be any praise, think on these things.

Philippians 4:8

Keep thy heart with all diligence; for out of it are the issues of life.

Proverbs 4:23

A good man out of the good treasure of the heart bringeth forth good things: and an evil man out of the evil treasure bringeth forth evil things.

Matthew 12:35

Poverty comes on people who don't think the way God thinks about money. We've got to walk in line with what God's Word says in order to be truly prosperous.

THE BLESSINGS OF DEUTERONOMY 28

"If you fully obey all of these commandments of the Lord your God, the laws I am declaring to you today, God will transform you into the greatest nation in the world. These are the blessings that will come upon you:

> *Blessings in the city,*
> *Blessings in the field;*
> *Many children,*
> *Ample crops,*
> *Large flocks and herds;*
> *Blessings of fruit and bread;*
> *Blessings when you come in,*
> *Blessings when you go out.*

"The Lord will defeat your enemies before you; they will march out together against you but scatter before you in seven directions! The Lord will bless you with good crops and healthy cattle, and prosper everything you do when you arrive in the land the Lord your God is giving you. He will change you into a holy people dedicated to himself; this he has promised to do if you will only obey him and walk in his ways. All the nations in the world shall see that you belong to the Lord, and they will stand in awe.

"The Lord will give you an abundance of good things in the land, just as he promised: many children, many cattle, and abundant crops. He will open to you his wonderful treasury of rain in the heavens, to give you fine crops every season. He will bless everything you do; and you shall lend to many nations, but shall not borrow from them. If you will only listen and obey the commandments of the Lord your God that I am giving you today, he will make you the head and not the tail, and you shall always have the upper hand. But each of these blessings depends on your not turning aside in any way from the laws I have given you; and you must never worship other gods."

Deuteronomy 28:1-14 TLB

That's one of the most powerful passages of scripture! When we obey God's Word and get prosperity down on the inside of us, it will show up in our pocketbooks. We'll get opportunities to make more money. We'll have to work, believe God and resist the devil, but God wants us to prosper. He wants His people to be blessed.

WEALTH WORDS FROM THE BIBLE
WEALTH

Praise ye the LORD. Blessed is the man that feareth the LORD, that delighteth greatly in his commandments. His seed shall be mighty upon earth: the generation of the upright shall be blessed. Wealth and riches shall be in his house: and his righteousness endureth for ever.

Psalm 112:1-3

But thou shalt remember the LORD thy God: for it is he that giveth thee power to get wealth, that he may establish his covenant which he sware unto thy fathers, as it is this day.

Deuteronomy 8:18

Moreover, when God gives any man wealth and possessions, and enables him to enjoy them, to accept his lot and be happy in his work—this is a gift of God. He seldom reflects on the days of his life, because God keeps him occupied with gladness of heart.

Ecclesiastes 5:19-20 NIV

RICHES

Happy is the man that findeth wisdom, and the man that getteth understanding. For the merchandise of it is better than the merchandise of silver, and the gain thereof than fine gold. She is more precious than rubies: and all the things thou canst desire are not to be compared unto her. Length of days is in her right hand; and in her left hand riches and honour.

Proverbs 3:13-16

By humility and the fear of the LORD are riches, and honour, and life.

Proverbs 22:4

Through wisdom is an house builded; and by understanding it is established: And by knowledge shall the chambers be filled with all precious and pleasant riches.

Proverbs 24:3-4

PROSPERITY

Let them shout for joy, and be glad, that favour my righteous cause: yea, let them say continually, Let the LORD be magnified, which hath pleasure in the prosperity of his servant.

Psalm 35:27

Save now, I beseech thee, O LORD: O LORD, I beseech thee, send now prosperity.

Psalm 118:25

Pray for the peace of Jerusalem: they shall prosper that love thee.

Psalm 122:6

ABUNDANCE

The thief cometh not, but for to steal, and to kill, and to destroy: I am come that they might have life, and that they might have it more abundantly.

John 10:10

For the LORD has chosen Zion, he has desired it for his dwelling: "This is my resting place for ever and ever; here I will sit enthroned, for I have desired it—I will bless her with abundant provisions; her poor will I satisfy with food."

                                                    Psalm 132:13-15 NIV

Now unto him that is able to do exceeding abundantly above all that we ask or think, according to the power that worketh in us...

                                                    Ephesians 3:20

INCREASE

A wise man will hear, and will increase learning; and a man of understanding shall attain unto wise counsels...

                                                    Proverbs 1:5

The LORD shall increase you more and more, you and your children. Ye are blessed of the LORD which made heaven and earth.

                                                    Psalm 115:14-15

Wealth gotten by vanity shall be diminished: but he that gathereth by labour shall increase.

                                                    Proverbs 13:11

SATISFIED

The LORD knoweth the days of the upright: and their inheritance shall be for ever. They shall not be ashamed in the evil time: and in the days of famine they shall be satisfied.

                                                    Psalm 37:18-19

He that tilleth his land shall be satisfied with bread: but he that followeth vain persons is void of understanding.

                                                    Proverbs 12:11

Be glad then, ye children of Zion, and rejoice in the LORD your God: for he hath given you the former rain moderately, and he will cause to come down for you the rain, the former rain, and the latter rain in the first month. And the floors shall be full of wheat, and the fats shall overflow with wine and oil. And I will restore to you the years that the locust hath eaten, the cankerworm, and the caterpiller, and the palmerworm, my great army which I sent among you. And ye shall eat in plenty, and be satisfied, and praise the name of the LORD your God, that hath dealt wondrously with you: and my people shall never be ashamed.

                                                    Joel 2:23-26

LACK

The young lions do lack, and suffer hunger: but they that seek the LORD shall not want any good thing.

Psalm 34:10

He that giveth unto the poor shall not lack: but he that hideth his eyes shall have many a curse.

Proverbs 28:27

The LORD is my shepherd; I shall not want.

Psalm 23:1

NEED

Be not ye therefore like unto them: for your Father knoweth what things ye have need of, before ye ask him.

Matthew 6:8

And seek not ye what ye shall eat, or what ye shall drink, neither be ye of doubtful mind. For all these things do the nations of the world seek after: and your Father knoweth that ye have need of these things. But rather seek ye the kingdom of God; and all these things shall be added unto you.

Luke 12:29-31

But my God shall supply all your need according to his riches in glory by Christ Jesus.

Philippians 4:19

POOR

This poor man cried, and the LORD heard him, and saved him out of all his troubles.

Psalm 34:6

All my bones shall say, LORD, who is like unto thee, which deliverest the poor from him that is too strong for him, yea, the poor and the needy from him that spoileth him?

Psalm 35:10

He shall deliver the needy when he crieth; the poor also, and him that hath no helper.

Psalm 72:12

RICH

He becometh poor that dealeth with a slack hand: but the hand of the diligent maketh rich.

Proverbs 10:4

The wealth of the rich is their fortified city, but poverty is the ruin of the poor.
Proverbs 10:15 NIV

The blessing of the LORD, it maketh rich, and he addeth no sorrow with it.
Proverbs 10:22

The rich ruleth over the poor, and the borrower is servant to the lender.
Proverbs 22:7

For you know the grace of our Lord Jesus Christ, that though he was rich, yet for your sakes he became poor, so that you through his poverty might become rich.
II Corinthians 8:9 NIV

BUDGET

For which of you, intending to build a tower, sitteth not down first, and counteth the cost, whether he have sufficient to finish it? Lest haply, after he hath laid the foundation, and is not able to finish it, all that behold it begin to mock him, Saying, This man began to build, and was not able to finish.
Luke 14:28-30

Be thou diligent to know the state of thy flocks, and look well to thy herds.
Proverbs 27:23

Now about the collection for God's people: Do what I told the Galatian churches to do. On the first day of every week, each one of you should set aside a sum of money in keeping with his income, saving it up, so that when I come no collections will have to be made.
I Corinthians 16:1-2 NIV

STEWARDSHIP

"The master commended the dishonest manager because he had acted shrewdly. For the people of this world are more shrewd in dealing with their own kind than are the people of the light. I tell you, use worldly wealth to gain friends for yourselves, so that when it is gone, you will be welcomed into eternal dwellings.
Luke 16:8-9 NIV

And the Lord said, Who then is that faithful and wise steward, whom his lord shall make ruler over his household, to give them their portion of meat in due season? Blessed is that servant, whom his lord when he cometh shall find so doing.

Of a truth I say unto you, that he will make him ruler over all that he hath.

Luke 12:42-44

Moreover it is required in stewards, that a man be found faithful.

I Corinthians 4:2

As every man hath received the gift, even so minister the same one to another, as good stewards of the manifold grace of God.

I Peter 4:10

THE STORY OF JABEZ

In his book *The Prayer Of Jabez,* (Sisters, OR: Multnomah Publishing, 2000), Bruce Wilkinson writes in depth on the subject of the prayer of a man in the Bible named Jabez.

Although the story of Jabez is only two verses long in the Bible, Wilkinson points out that Jabez was a man who wanted to be all he could be and a man who wanted to do as much as he could for the Lord.

Now Jabez was more honorable than his brothers, and his mother called his name Jabez, saying, "Because I bore him in pain." And Jabez called on the God of Israel, saying, "Oh that thou wouldest bless me indeed, and enlarge my territory, that Your hand would be with me, and that You would keep me from evil, that I may not cause pain!" So God granted him what he requested.

I Chronicles 4:9-10 NKJV

God granted the request of Jabez, and we can learn something very important from the prayer that he prayed.

God wants us to ask Him for more blessing, more territory, more favor and safekeeping from evil.

$ection 2

financial house cleaning
Order Precedes Increase

financial
house cleaning

ORDER PRECEDES INCREASE

WHAT WE NEED:

Financial order—God does everything decently and in order.

WHY WE NEED IT:

Destruction comes from a lack of knowledge, and where there is no plan, we will surely perish.

HOW DO WE ACCOMPLISH ORDER?

- We must create a spending plan (a budget).

- We must find out how to spend less and save more.

- We need to manage our credit and get out of debt.

In this section, we're going to get our financial houses in order. Successful planning involves knowing where we are starting from, knowing where we want to end up, and having a system in place to monitor our progress along the way.

> *Any enterprise is built by wise planning, becomes strong through common sense, and profits wonderfully by keeping abreast of the facts.*
> *Proverbs 24:3-4 TLB*

MATH AND MONEY

If we weren't good students in school when it came to the subject of math, there's a pretty good chance that we aren't automatically going to be good managers of our money either. Why is that?

It's because, math represents money.

We can't just hide our heads in the sand and say, "We don't need to learn this stuff." No, we'll go broke doing that. Math is important for survival in this world. We need to understand that a lot of things in the kingdom of God are tied to math.

Think about the story of Noah's Ark in Genesis 6. God said, "Noah make yourself a boat out of cypress wood. This is how you need to build it. Make it 450 feet long, 75 feet wide, and 45 feet high, etc." God was very specific on how big the Ark should be and how it should be designed.

If Noah had not followed the instructions God gave him, that boat would have sunk. God knew exactly how many animals and people were going to be on the Ark. He knew the weight of the boat and its contents and the intensity of the flood. There was a TV special years ago, where someone built a scale-model replica of the Ark and tried to estimate its weight. Then they put the model in a wave pool and tried to sink it. Their conclusion was that the Ark was virtually unsinkable because of its dimensions. ***God knows something about math.***

All throughout scripture we are faced with the concept of mathematics. Here are just a few references to look up:

- Luke 16:9—Make money a friend.

- Matthew 25:14-30—God is a God of stewardship.

- II Kings 4:1—We can love God and still be broke.

- Luke 12:7—The hairs of our heads are numbered.

- Proverbs 27:23—We need to know the condition of our flocks.

- Proverbs 11:1—The Lord hates dishonest scales, but accurate scales are His delight.

- Acts 5:1-10—Ananias and Sapphira lied and died because of money.

- Luke 9:14—Order precedes increase.

- Psalm 90:10, 12—The days of our lives are numbered.

- Proverbs 9:11—The lengths of our lives can be multiplied and increased.

- Exodus 25-27—God cares about the smallest details.

DEVELOP A LOVE OF MATH

- An inscription over the door of Plato's Academy in Athens read: "Let no one enter here who is ignorant of geometry."

- Mathematics leads to higher education.

- More and more good jobs require math skills.

- Cooking, shopping, household budgets and interpreting mutual fund reports all require skills in math.

- Math demands clarity in thought.

- Math is necessary for problem solving.

- Only in three countries—Lithuania, Cyprus and South Africa—do students score lower than American twelfth graders in math. *Not surprisingly, America is the number-one debtor nation on earth!*

ORDER PRECEDES INCREASE

It's a spiritual principle in the kingdom of God that order precedes increase. Natural steps lead to supernatural increase and blessing.

God directed Noah to take some very precise, natural steps before the supernatural saving during the flood could take place. It was the same way with Moses and the Tabernacle and the priests and the Temple. Until they were built and furnished to God's exact specifications, the glory of God did not come down on them. In II Kings 4, when the widow said to Elisha, "I'm in debt, Preacher. What am I going to do?" the prophet answered her with a question: "What can you do?"

Order precedes increase. God is always going to ask us to do something natural before He'll do something supernatural.

So if we're going to see the supernatural in our financial lives, we're going to have to prepare for it in the natural. Just look at what God's Word has to say about preparation.

Prepare thy work without, and make it fit for thyself in the field; and afterwards build thine house.

Proverbs 24:27

The ants are a people not strong, yet they prepare their meat in the summer.

Proverbs 30:25

Thou preparest a table before me in the presence of mine enemies: thou anointest my head with oil; my cup runneth over.

Psalm 23:5

We've got to get our lives in order, if we want to have the blessings of God in our homes, our relationships and our finances.

ORGANIZATIONAL SKILLS AND TIME MANAGEMENT

To manage our money effectively, we're going to have to learn to manage our time. We can't get more than 24 hours in a day—and a certain amount of that time has to be devoted to eating and sleeping, etc., to survive. So if we want increase, we're going to have to become skilled in organization and time management. We've got to learn to use our 24 hours each day better.

Let all things be done decently and in order.

I Corinthians 14:40

For this cause left I thee in Crete, that thou shouldest set in order the things that are wanting, and ordain elders in every city, as I had appointed thee.

Titus 1:5

So teach us to number our days, that we may apply our hearts unto wisdom.

Psalm 90:12

To every thing there is a season, and a time to every purpose under the heaven: A time

to be born	*to die*
to plant	*to pluck up that which is planted*
to kill	*to heal*
to break down	*to build up*
to weep	*to laugh*
to mourn	*to dance*
to cast away stones	*to gather stones together*
to embrace	*to refrain from embracing*
to get	*to lose*
to keep	*to cast away*
to rend	*to sew*

to keep silence   to speak
to love   to hate
of war   of peace
He hath made every thing beautiful in his time....

Ecclesiastes 3:1-8, 11

"I, Wisdom, will make the hours of your day more profitable and the years of your life more fruitful."

Proverbs 9:11 TLB

Commit thy works unto the LORD, and thy thoughts shall be established. A man's heart deviseth his way: but the LORD directeth his steps.

Proverbs 16:3, 9

The steps of a good man are ordered by the LORD: and he delighteth in his way.

Psalm 37:23

For as many as are led by the Spirit of God, they are the sons of God.

Romans 8:14

GOD KEEPS RECORDS

Did you know that God keeps records?

The Bible says that when we get to Heaven, we're going to have to give an account of every idle word we've spoken and every idle deed we've done. God has everything He owns inventoried. There are even counting angels who count everything, including the hairs of our heads. Every time a bird falls out of tree, an angel writes it down. God knows where all of His stuff is at any given moment.

Whatever is has already been, and what will be has been before; and God will call the past to account.

Ecclesiastes 3:15 NIV

So then every one of us shall give account of himself to God.

Romans 14:12

But I say unto you, That every idle word that men shall speak, they shall give account thereof in the day of judgment.

Matthew 12:36

Obey them that have the rule over you, and submit yourselves: for they watch for your souls, as they that must give account....

Hebrews 13:17

But they will have to give account to him who is ready to judge the living and the dead.

I Peter 4:5 NIV

Not because I desire a gift: but I desire fruit that may abound to your account.

Philippians 4:17

Then they that feared the LORD spake often one to another: and the LORD hearkened, and heard it, and a book of remembrance was written before him for them that feared the LORD, and that thought upon his name.

Malachi 3:16

Thine eyes did see my substance, yet being unperfect; and in thy book all my members were written, which in continuance were fashioned, when as yet there was none of them.

Psalm 139:16

Let them be blotted out of the book of the living, and not be written with the righteous.

Psalm 69:28

And I saw the dead, small and great, stand before God; and the books were opened: and another book was opened, which is the book of life: and the dead were judged out of those things which were written in the books, according to their works.

Revelation 20:12

FIVE PRINCIPLES OF FINANCIAL SECURITY

There are five principles of financial security in the Word of God. They will never go away. We're going to have to practice them the rest of our lives.

Principle #1—Keep Good Records.

We've got to find out what we own and what we owe. We have to find out what we earn and where it goes. To do that, we're going to have to keep some good records. *(I'll cover how to do this in detail a little later.)* Stewardship involves record keeping.

What if we went into a restaurant and asked the waitress for a menu and she said, "We don't have a menu. We've just got a lot of food back there, but I don't really know what we have"? That would be crazy.

Would a family ever just get in their car, have it loaded up to go on vacation and then say, "Where are we going? Oh, let's just take off in some direction"? Of course not.

In the same way, we need to know how much cash we have in our pockets and how much we have in the bank. Before we buy a meal, before we buy a car, before we buy a house, we've got to know, "Can we afford this?"

> *Get the facts at any price and hold on tightly to all the good sense you can get.*
> *Proverbs 23:23 TLB*

Get the facts at any price! If someone were coming to see me and they were in financial trouble, the first thing I would tell them is, "Go home and get all your paperwork and bring it to me. I can't take you where you need to go financially until I find out where you are."

> *Be thou diligent to know the state of thy flocks, and look well to thy herds.*
> *Proverbs 27:23*

God says to us, "I do supernatural things. I made the earth. I made animals. I made sheep. I made grass. I make rain. I make rain fall. I make grass grow. I make sheep get fat." Then He tells us, "But once you go down to the marketplace, you're on your own. When you go to sell your sheep, you'd better know the condition of your herds and the state of your flocks. You'd better know how fat those sheep are and how thick that wool is. You'd better know the going price for wool. You'd better know the going rate for sheep, because if you don't, somebody's going to clean your plow at the marketplace."

Before we buy a car, we've got to know what that car is worth. What kind of loan can we get on it? What's the resale value of it? What's the insurance going to cost? God says, we'd better take care to know the condition of our flocks, our herds, our cars, our houses, our finances. That's our job. We're responsible for natural things. He does supernatural things.

To see increase in our lives, we're going to have to take some time—a day, a week, a month—however long it takes—to get our stuff together. Then we'll have a great idea of where we are so we can begin to do something.

Faith is based on fact, not on fiction. We need to find out where we are, so we can begin to do something to get to where we want to go.

Principle #2—Tithe And Give.

All the laws of God concerning sowing, reaping and increase involve two things for a Christian—tithing and giving.

> *Honour the LORD with thy substance, and with the firstfruits of all thine*
> *increase: So shall thy barns be filled with plenty, and thy presses shall burst out*

with new wine.

Proverbs 3:9-10

If we honor the Lord with our first fruits, He'll see that we're taken care of. We can't get back what we haven't sown. When we pay our tithes, we're not paying Him something we own. God already owns everything.

We just manage God's stuff. We don't own a thing. We don't have to worry about being rich, because we don't own it. The Bible says we didn't bring it with us when we came, and we don't take it with us when we leave. God owns it all and we're simply managers of His stuff. The better we manage it, the more we get to manage.

God says we determine how much we have. If we make sure that we pay Him the tenth, He'll multiply our 90%, because He sees that we fear and honor Him. We won't have to worry about a thing. *(We'll be covering this subject later in Section Four.)*

> *One man gives freely, yet gains even more; another withholds unduly, but comes to poverty. A generous man will prosper; he who refreshes others will himself be refreshed.*
>
> *Proverbs 11:24-25 NIV*

The way we get more is by sowing more. We sow and we reap, so we can sow again. Giving has to become a lifestyle.

Principle #3—Save For The Future.

Most Christians—people who know the Word and the Spirit of God—still somehow struggle with saving for the future.

> *Go to the ant, you sluggard; consider its ways and be wise! It has no commander, no overseer or ruler, yet it stores its provisions in summer and gathers its food at harvest.*
>
> *Proverbs 6:6-8 NIV*

In other words, an ant, even though it doesn't have a boss, a leader or a book to read has enough sense to know it won't be summer forever. Eventually winter comes. Eventually the harvest is past. So we'd better lay up some money, not only enough for today, but enough for the future.

> *Dishonest money dwindles away, but he who gathers money little by little makes it grow.*
>
> *Proverbs 13:11 NIV*

How do we save for the future?

We do it a little at a time. God doesn't expect us to put $1,000 a day into the bank, or even a $100 a day. But He does expect us to put something back.

Paul, who wrote two-thirds of the New Testament, understood the concept of saving for the future (I Corinthians 16:1-2). We need to be setting some money aside for the future. We can do it for a special offering. We can do it for a used car. We can do it for retirement. We can do it for Christmas. It is a principle in the Word of God to put money back for the future.

> *Blessed shall be thy basket and thy store.*
>
> *Deuteronomy 28:5*

God says He'll bless us in our storehouse, but He can't do it unless we've got one—even if it's just a simple savings account. We've got to save for the future.

Principle #4—Have A Spending Plan.

A lot of people get uncomfortable when they hear the word "budget," but having a spending plan involves some tremendous spiritual laws. Good planning and hard work lead to prosperity.

> *Steady plodding brings prosperity; hasty speculation brings poverty.*
>
> *Proverbs 21:5 TLB*

Every successful corporation has a five-year business plan. Every family ought to have a five-year business plan, too.

> *"But don't begin until you count the cost. For who would begin construction of a building without first getting estimates and then checking to see if he has enough money to pay the bills? Otherwise he might complete only the foundation before running out of funds. And then how everyone would laugh! "'See that fellow there?' they would mock. 'He started that building and ran out of money before it was finished!'"*
>
> *Luke 14:28-30 TLB*

There's no honor in our work when we start something we can't finish.

> *Remove far from me vanity and lies: give me neither poverty nor riches; feed me with food convenient for me: Lest I be full, and deny thee, and say, Who is the LORD? or lest I be poor, and steal, and take the name of my God in vain.*
>
> *Proverbs 30:8-9*

Now, some people have quoted this and said, "See, God doesn't want us to have any money. He wants us to have just enough."

But they don't understand. They've missed the whole point.

The point of this scripture is that we're supposed to glorify God with the money we've got. If all we do is hoard up money and don't use it to bring God glory, we've made money a god, and we've fallen into the snare of the devil.

There's only one reason you and I need money: It's to help us fulfill God's plan for our lives. If we do what God has called us to do, it brings God glory. So, the first thing we have to do is find out why God put us here. Then we need to use our financial resources to accomplish His plans and purposes for ourselves, our businesses, our ministries and our families.

Why are we here on this planet, and what are we supposed to be doing?

We need to find out, because we need *X* number of dollars to do the job we've been called to do.

We can look at the past and do it for people who have died. We can say, "This person spent this much money, he built this kind of business, and he built this many buildings." We can see how much he earned, what he spent and how much he left behind. So certainly, we can do it for the future.

In my spending plan—the plan God has for Joe McGee—I've got to find my number. If I'm going to glorify God and fulfill what He wants me to do in this world, how much money do I need?

I can find that number by doing the math.

First, I'm called to provide for my wife and my six children. Well, according to the government, there's a number, and if we're just average, I know I'm already going to need more than $1 million just to raise my six kids. That's not for me and my wife. That's not for my retirement. That's just for my kids.

Using the rate of inflation, I can estimate about how much money it's going to take to provide for my family and to make sure my house is paid for by the time I'm 65. I can estimate the annual cost of all of our food, clothing, bills, etc., after I retire, and I can add those up, too. That gives me a number.

Then, since I'm called to have a ministry, I know I need to have buildings, I need to pay salaries, I've got to maintain lights, produce tapes and books and pay for radio programs and television. All I have to do is sit down with a calculator and a note pad, and I can estimate the cost of what I think it's going to take to build this ministry the way I believe God wants it to be. There is a number for all I'm going to need.

Sometimes that number might seem scary. I may think, "How am I ever going to come up with that much money?" But if I don't find out the amount I need, I can't take steps to fulfill God's plan for Joe McGee here on earth.

It's not that I just want money for money's sake. I need money—a certain amount of it—as a tool to do what I'm called to do.

Everyone has a different number, based on God's plans for them. If we don't find out what we're going to need, we'll fall into a trap.

> *Then he gave an illustration: "A rich man had a fertile farm that produced fine crops. In fact, his barns were full to overflowing—he couldn't get everything in. He thought about his problem, and finally exclaimed, 'I know— I'll tear down my barns and build bigger ones! Then I'll have room enough. And I'll sit back and say to myself, "Friend, you have enough stored away for years to come. Now take it easy! Wine, women, and song for you!"' "But God said to him, 'Fool! Tonight you die. Then who will get it all?' "Yes, every man is a fool who gets rich on earth but not in heaven."*
>
> *Luke 12:16-21 TLB*

This man had no limits. His barns were full. His needs were more than met. He was blessed. But instead of becoming a giver, what did he do?

He just built himself bigger barns. He had no plan for what he was supposed to accomplish in his life. His trust was not in God. His trust was in his wealth—and that's what destroyed him.

If we don't have a spending plan—or a budget—then we don't have any limits. We'll just spend and spend and spend. We'll shop 'til we drop, and then somebody else will get all our stuff.

Principle #5—Enjoy What You Have.

All the money in the world won't buy us happiness.

> *Stay away from the love of money; be satisfied with what you have. For God has said, "I will never, never fail you nor forsake you." That is why we can say without any doubt or fear, "The Lord is my Helper and I am not afraid of anything that mere man can do to me."*
>
> *Hebrews 13:5-6 TLB*

We need to be content with what we have right now—not because we're poor— but because we know we're not going to be poor forever. Even if we had millions of dollars in the bank today, having all that money wouldn't put happiness or joy in our souls.

I know how to live on almost nothing or with everything. I have learned the secret of contentment in every situation, whether it be a full stomach or hunger, plenty or want; for I can do everything God asks me to with the help of Christ who gives me the strength and power.

Philippians 4:12-13 TLB

Paul wasn't saying he was content to always have nothing. He was saying that he knew God was not going to leave him where he was. He knew God would give him the strength to change his circumstances.

How does God strengthen us?

He strengthens us when we meditate in His Word and speak it with our mouths (Joshua 1:7-8). As we fill our hearts and mouths with God's Word, we'll have the strength and the power to accomplish God's plans for our lives.

God is our source. We can be content whether we're living in a pup tent or in a mansion. He is our Helper. He'll never leave us or forsake us. He's our confidence. We don't have to be afraid of men, the boss down at the plant or what's going on in the economy, because God is going to take care of us.

Moreover, when God gives any man wealth and possessions, and enables him to enjoy them, to accept his lot and be happy in his work—this is a gift of God. He seldom reflects on the days of his life, because God keeps him occupied with gladness of heart.

Ecclesiastes 5:19-20 NIV

God is going to give us the power to get wealth and He's going to give us the ability to enjoy it. He's going to give us the ability to be happy in our work. That's His gift to us.

We should be so excited about what God is doing with us now and with what He's going to do with us in the future, that we won't think back on the "good old days." There won't be any "good old days" to think back on. The "good old days" are going to pale in comparison to the good day we're having today and to the great day we're going to have tomorrow. God is going to do great things for us!

GET YOUR FINANCIAL HOUSE IN ORDER

We need to get a cardboard box and collect up every bill, every contract, every policy, every check stub, every bank and credit card statement—everything we've got and get it all in one place. It doesn't matter if it's two years old, ten years old, or from last month. Once we get all our financial papers together in one place, then we can begin to separate everything.

Now don't panic! We can take a weekend, a week, a month, or two months, but we have to begin the process. If we want God to increase us financially, then we're going to have to become good stewards and create some order for what we already have.

Next, we need to get a file box or cabinet, ten hanging folders and a box of regular file folders to put inside them. We'll start by putting labels on the ten hanging folders.

1. **Checking And Savings Accounts**—This is where we keep our monthly bank statements and cancelled checks. We should use separate file folders inside the hanging folder, if we have different accounts.

2. **Home-Related Accounts**—Within this hanging folder, in separate files, we should put the title to our house, all home improvement receipts, mortgage payment receipts and paid utility bills. (Renters should keep copies of their leases and receipts for deposits and rent payments here.)

3. **Credit Cards/Loans And Other Debt**—We need to create separate files for each credit card account we have and keep all the bills, payment receipts and card agreements inside. We also need to keep all records of loans or debts other than our mortgage in separate files in here. Each file should have the loan agreement and the payment records in it.

4. **Insurance**—We should make a separate file for each of our policies (i.e., life, health, disability, homeowner's or renter's, etc.). The policies, notifications, and the related payment records need to go in the appropriate files.

5. **Taxes**—Since the law allows the IRS to go back seven years for an audit, we need to make eight file folders—one for each of the past seven years, plus this year. In each of the files, we should put all our W-2 forms, 1099s, tithing and giving records, other tax records and a copy of that year's returns.

6. **Social Security Documents/Retirement Accounts**—Our most recent Benefits Statements go in one file inside this hanging folder. (We can call the local Social Security office to request them.) Then we should make files for every retirement account we have, including IRAs, 401(k)s, 403(b)s, etc., and keep our quarterly statements inside them.

7. **Investments**—Papers with the amounts we originally paid for any investments (not retirement accounts), such as stocks or mutual funds

and the dates we bought or received them, as well as any dividend statements on them, go in here filed by date.

If any of the investments were inherited, we need to keep a record of their value on the date we got them in this file. That way if we want to look at selling them at some point in the future, we'll have the information we need to determine what our tax consequences will be ahead of time.

We also need to keep a paper in this file with the location of where these investments are kept, (i.e., original stock certificates and Grandpa's rare stamp collection in the safety deposit box, etc.).

8. **Estate And Legal Documents**—This hanging folder should have a copy of our most recent wills or trusts, medical directives, and power of attorney papers, along with the name, address and phone number of the attorney who set them up.

9. **Children's Accounts**—College savings plan papers, college loans, tuition records, and/or other investments or debts for the kids should go in this folder in separate files.

10. **Financial Worksheets**—A copy of our family's financial goals and a prayer list, as well as a worksheet of our net worth, a copy of our current spending plan, and our other financial worksheets should be included in this file. *(I've included a few simple worksheets in the next section to help you get started.)*

By now, you're thinking, "Man, this is going to take some time!"

You're right!

We can't do all this in one Saturday. But we have to stop putting it off and just start. Once it's done, we'll never sleep so good in our lives. This is a righteous thing to do for ourselves and for our families. It's scriptural for us to become good stewards over the things God has given us.

HELPFUL WORKSHEETS

1. How Much Do You Own?

2. How Much Do You Earn?

3. How Much Do You Owe?

4.   Where Does It Go?

Most people just don't realize all the hidden things that they're paying for each month. Take for example real estate taxes and homeowner's insurance. Many people don't really plan for those things adequately because they're lumped in with the house payment.

"So who cares?"

Well, we should, because we could be paying too much. We may need to change insurance companies or go down to the courthouse and have our property taxes re-evaluated.

How much do we spend on clothing, or our vacation, or on Christmas presents every year?

Most people don't really think about those things, or they think about them as one lump sum, but we ought to divide the amounts by twelve and start saving money every month so we can cover things ahead of time.

For example, the average American household spends about $2,500 in home repairs every year, so we'd better divide that by twelve and budget for it. It's going to take about $210 a month to keep our homes and the things in them in good repair.

Are we going to replace the couch in the next year? If not, we don't need to worry about it.

Is the washing machine fifteen years old? We might want to consider that.

Are we going to need new tires?

Are the kids going to need braces?

Food, car payments, gasoline, insurance, dry cleaning, optometrists, school supplies—*What are we actually spending?*

The key is to find the truth so we can really use our faith when we pray. Instead of saying, "Lord, bless our finances," we can pray, "Lord, thank You in advance for an extra $210 a month to keep the home You gave us in good repair. Thank You for helping us to prepare in advance for our needs."

When we get everything down on paper, it will help us make wise decisions. "Do we want to continue to do some of these things, or is there something else that's more important right now?"

If we'll take the natural steps to become better stewards of what God has given us, we'll begin to see increase come our way. Armed with the truth, we'll be able to see where we are now financially and what steps we need to take to fulfill what God has for us in the future.

On the following pages, you'll find some basic worksheets to help you find out what you have and where you are financially. Once you have all your financial files in order, you should be able to find all of this information fairly quickly.

Remember to file copies of these worksheets in your Financial Worksheets folder. Knowing where your money goes is a huge part of taking control of it. And one of the best gifts you can give yourself and your family is a well-organized system of keeping your financial records in one place.

HOW MUCH DO YOU OWN? (NET WORTH WORKSHEET)

ITEM DESCRIPTION	VALUE	–	DEBT	=	EQUITY
Real Estate _____	_____		_____		_____
Real Estate _____	_____		_____		_____
Vehicle _____	_____		_____		_____
Vehicle _____	_____		_____		_____
Vehicle _____	_____		_____		_____
Checking Acct _____	_____		_____		_____
Savings Acct _____	_____		_____		_____
Other Bank Acct _____	_____		_____		_____
Other Bank Acct _____	_____		_____		_____
Retirement Plan _____	_____		_____		_____
Retirement Plan _____	_____		_____		_____
Mutual Funds _____	_____		_____		_____
Mutual Funds _____	_____		_____		_____
Stocks/Bonds _____	_____		_____		_____
Stocks/Bonds _____	_____		_____		_____
Stocks/Bonds _____	_____		_____		_____
Whole Life Insurance _____	_____		_____		_____
Furnishings _____	_____		_____		_____
Equipment _____	_____		_____		_____
Jewelry _____	_____		_____		_____
Antiques _____	_____		_____		_____
Unsecured Debt (Negative) _____	_____		_____		_____
Credit Card Debt (Negative) _____	_____		_____		_____
Other _____	_____		_____		_____
Other _____	_____		_____		_____
Other _____	_____		_____		_____
TOTAL NET WORTH_____	_____	–	_____	=	_____

HOW MUCH DO YOU EARN? (INCOME WORKSHEET)

INCOME	MONTHLY AMOUNT	ANNUAL AMOUNT
Wages	_____	_____
Wages	_____	_____
Wages	_____	_____
Reimbursed Expenses	_____	_____
Interest Income	_____	_____
Dividend Income	_____	_____
Rents Paid To You	_____	_____
Notes Paid To You	_____	_____
Alimony	_____	_____
Child Support	_____	_____
Social Security Distributions	_____	_____
Other Distributions	_____	_____
Disability/Unemployment	_____	_____
Cash Gifts To You	_____	_____
Other _____	_____	_____
Other _____	_____	_____
Other _____	_____	_____
Other _____	_____	_____
Other _____	_____	_____
Other _____	_____	_____
Other _____	_____	_____
TOTAL INCOME	_____	_____

HOW MUCH DO YOU OWE? (CURRENT EXPENSES)

ITEM DESCRIPTION	MONTHLY AMOUNT	ANNUAL AMOUNT
Tithes/Offerings	_____	_____
Income Taxes	_____	_____
Mortgage Principal & Interest	_____	_____
Real Estate Taxes	_____	_____
Homeowner's Insurance	_____	_____
Home Repairs/Services	_____	_____
Replace Home Furnishings	_____	_____
Utilities	_____	_____
Groceries And Restaurants	_____	_____
Medical Bills/Payments	_____	_____
Health Insurance	_____	_____
Life Insurance	_____	_____
Disability Insurance	_____	_____
Car Payment(s)	_____	_____
Car Insurance	_____	_____
Car Fuel/Repairs/Tags	_____	_____
Replace Car	_____	_____
Clothing	_____	_____
Child Care	_____	_____
Tuition	_____	_____
All Loan Payments	_____	_____
All Credit Card Payments	_____	_____
All Other Debt Payments	_____	_____
Vacation	_____	_____
Gifts	_____	_____
Entertainment_____	_____	_____
Other _____	_____	_____
Other _____	_____	_____
Other _____	_____	_____
TOTAL EXPENSES	_____	_____

WHERE DOES IT GO? (SPENDING PLAN)

CATEGORY	BUDGETED	SUBTOTAL
Giving		
Tithe	_____	
Offerings	_____	
		_____
Savings		
Emergency Fund	_____	
Retirement Fund	_____	
College Fund	_____	
		_____
Housing		
Mortgage Principal & Interest	_____	
Real Estate Taxes	_____	
Homeowner's Insurance	_____	
Home Repairs	_____	
Replace Furniture	_____	
Utilities	_____	
		_____
Food		
Groceries	_____	
Restaurants	_____	
		_____
Transportation		
Total Vehicle Payments	_____	
Fuel	_____	
Repairs/Tags	_____	
Vehicle Insurance	_____	
Car Replacement	_____	
		_____
Clothing		
Total Clothing Purchases	_____	
Cleaning/Laundry	_____	
		_____

CATEGORY	BUDGETED	SUBTOTAL

Medical/Health

Health Insurance   _____

Life Insurance   _____

Disability Insurance   _____

Doctor Bills/Payments   _____

Medicine   _____

                                              _____

Miscellaneous Expenses

Child Care   _____

Tuition/Student Loans   _____

Dues & Subscriptions   _____

Vacation   _____

Gifts   _____

Entertainment   _____

Other _____   _____

Other _____   _____

                                              _____

Other Debts

Credit Card _____   _____

Credit Card _____   _____

Credit Card _____   _____

Credit Card _____   _____

Other Debts _____   _____

Other Debts _____   _____

Other Debts _____   _____

                                              _____

GRAND TOTAL MONTHLY EXPENSES   _____

TOTAL MONTHLY INCOME   _____

LESS TOTAL MONTHLY EXPENSES   – _____

BALANCE LEFT OVER (OR AMOUNT SHORT) = _____

AVERAGE EXPENDITURE COMPARISON WORKSHEET

Our Household Income   _____/Month   _____/Year

U.S. Average Expenditure Pattern Compared To Our Home:

ITEM (U.S. AVG %)	AMT/MO	AMT/YR	OUR %
Housing* (32.9%)	_____	_____	_____
Includes Utilities (6.9%)			
Includes Furnishings/Equipment (3.7%)			
Transportation (19.1%)	_____	_____	_____
Personal Insurance/Pensions (9.9%)	_____	_____	_____
Food At Home (7.7%)	_____	_____	_____
Health Care (5.9%)	_____	_____	_____
Food Away From Home (5.4%)	_____	_____	_____
Apparel Products And Services (4%)	_____	_____	_____
Entertainment (1.9%)	_____	_____	_____
Education (1.9%)	_____	_____	_____
Alcoholic Beverages (1%)	_____	_____	_____
Tobacco Products (0.7%)	_____	_____	_____

Please Note: These percentages are what the average American household spends. *I am not telling you this is what you need to be spending.* Don't try to make your numbers fit what the average American household spends.

Your circumstances may be different. The average American household has 1.2 kids. You might have six kids, so some of these numbers wouldn't be realistic for you. The average American household spends 1% on alcohol and 0.7% on tobacco. If you don't smoke and you don't drink, you've already saved almost 2% of your budget, so you can apply that money somewhere else.

This worksheet is simply designed to give you an idea of where you are financially. Are you spending more than the average household in a certain category? Do you have a legitimate reason?

If you do, don't worry about it. If you don't have a good reason, you need to look at why you're spending more and re-evaluate where your money should be going.

CREDIT CARD STATISTICS

1. The average American adult received seven credit card offers through the mail last year, regardless of their credit history. *(To stop unsolicited credit card offers and possibly keep someone from stealing your identity by opening a pre-approved card in your name, call 1-888-5-OPT-OUT.)*

2. The average family in credit card debt carries a balance of $4,000 on several cards from month to month.

3. If you didn't have your credit card payment of $400 a month, and you invested that money in a tax-deferred savings plan paying 11% interest instead, in 30 years you could retire with $1.1 million in the bank. Credit card payments cost thousands of dollars in interest, keep many Americans from saving for their retirement and make bankruptcy look like a good alternative.

4. In 2002, over 1.3 million Americans filed for bankruptcy—the highest number in our nation's history.

5. The average credit limit on a credit card is $7,000.

6. The average interest rate is 18.9%.

7. Average late payment fees on a credit card are now $29-$35. Late fees totalled $7.7 billion in 2003, plus credit card issuers regularly hike the interest rates on their cards after receiving just one late payment.

8. The average American household has ten credit cards!

9. Almost half the households in America report having difficulty paying their minimum monthly payments.

10. If your credit card balance is $8,000, and you make the minimum monthly payment at 18% interest, it will take you 25 years and 7 months to pay the debt off. You will pay $15,432 in interest charges (almost twice the balance), bringing your total amount paid to $23,432.

11. Americans paid out approximately ***$65 billion*** in interest in 2002 alone! (Do you know how much a billion dollars is? If you stacked up $1,000 bills, it would take a 12-inch stack to make one million dollars. BUT— if you stacked up the same $1,000 bills, it would take a stack as high as the Empire State Building to make just one billion dollars!!)

12. To calculate your Debt-To-Income Ratio, divide your debt by your income. (A person making $40,000 a year gross income with $20,000 of outstanding debt has a 50% DTI Ratio.) If your DTI Ratio is over 45%, you'll be charged higher interest rates for loans. Lenders see you as "overextended."

13. The typical minimum monthly credit card payment is 90% interest and 10% principal.

14. Over three-fourths of Americans don't pay off their credit card each month, even though they swear they will.

SIGNS THAT YOU HAVE CREDIT CARD PROBLEMS

If any, or all, of these signs are present in your life, you're headed for disaster:

1. You pay only the minimum payment each month and don't know the total amount you owe on all your cards.

2. You use your credit card to pay for things you should never charge, like groceries.

3. You're at or near the credit limit of your card and have gone over it more than once in the past year.

4. You've been contacted more than once about missed or late payments.

5. If you didn't charge another dime, it would still take you a year or more to pay off your balance.

DEBT AND CREDIT HOUSE CLEANING
DEBT HOUSE CLEANING

> *Owe no man any thing, but to love one another: for he that loveth another hath fulfilled the law.*
>
> *Romans 13:8*

Americans have created $1 trillion worth of credit card debt. It's out of control! You and I had better be doing something different than the world is doing. We need to be led by the Spirit of God and use some wisdom concerning our money, or we're not going to have any.

So what should we do?

1. **Cut up the cards**—The average American has ten credit cards. That's eight or nine too many. We need one good credit card, like a Visa, MasterCard or American Express, and maybe a gas card for our gasoline. (But we shouldn't charge a Snickers or a drink when we go in to pay.)

2. **Be patient**—We didn't get into debt overnight and we can't get out overnight either. While we're working on paying off our debts, we can take those 2.9%-introductory-rate card offers and transfer the balances of our cards with the highest interest to the new lower-rate cards.

3. **Learn to say "no"**—If it's not on our spending plan, don't buy it. We should never go to the mall or the grocery store without a list. (People spend 25% more on stuff and 54% more on food when they use credit cards instead of cash.) If we have to use a card to buy something, we need to know exactly how we're going to pay it off before our next bill comes around.

4. **Comparison shop**—When we shop, we need to compare prices. Just because they put the cereal in a big box, doesn't mean it's cheaper than the cereal in a little box. We have to read the price-per-unit tag on the shelf!

5. **Buy at the right time**—In this section, under *Other Ways To Save Money*, I've listed when certain big-ticket items typically go on sale. We can save a whole lot of money, if we'll just learn to buy things in the right season. (That down parka will be 75% off in July!)

6. **Don't stay unemployed long**—If you don't have a job, get one and get it quick!

7. **Buy Quality**—Don't just buy what's cheap. We're going to buy three cheap things when we could have bought one quality item. Don't buy a cheap lawnmower. Buy a good one that will last several years. Learn to recognize quality and don't just look for the cheapest item.

8. **Create a debt-reduction plan**—We need to have a plan to get rid of our debts. The best way to do that is to list all our credit cards on a debt-payoff chart with what we owe, the interest rates, expiration dates, credit limits and available balances on each card. We should list any notes or loans we have, too.

    You can write down everything you owe on the debt-payoff chart on the next two pages.

To fill out this chart, we need to write in all the balances of our credit cards and loans (except our mortgage).

To start reducing our debt, we need to find the card or note with the lowest balance and double up our payments on it each month. (If we can't double our payments, we need to at least add something extra to be applied to the principal—even if it's just $10 a month.)

DEBT-PAYOFF CHART

CREDIT CARD (LOAN)	BALANCE	INTEREST	EXPIRATION
1 _____	_____	_____	_____
2 _____	_____	_____	_____
3 _____	_____	_____	_____
4 _____	_____	_____	_____
5 _____	_____	_____	_____
6 _____	_____	_____	_____
7 _____	_____	_____	_____
8 _____	_____	_____	_____
9 _____	_____	_____	_____
10 _____	_____	_____	_____
11 _____	_____	_____	_____
12 _____	_____	_____	_____
13 _____	_____	_____	_____
14 _____	_____	_____	_____
15 _____	_____	_____	_____
16 _____	_____	_____	_____
TOTAL DEBT	_____	_____	A.I.R.*

*Average Interest
Rate On All Accounts

As soon as that debt is paid off, we roll all the money we were paying on that first credit card or loan over to pay extra each month on the next biggest debt.

We keep paying the extra amount until that debt is paid off, and then we do the same for the next biggest debt, and the next one after that, etc. If we keep at it, we'll be surprised how quickly we can pay our debts down. Financial experts call this a "debt-payoff snowball."

CREDIT LIMIT	AVAILABLE BALANCE	NOTES
1 _____	_____	_____
2 _____	_____	_____
3 _____	_____	_____
4 _____	_____	_____
5 _____	_____	_____
6 _____	_____	_____
7 _____	_____	_____
8 _____	_____	_____
9 _____	_____	_____
10 _____	_____	_____
11 _____	_____	_____
12 _____	_____	_____
13 _____	_____	_____
14 _____	_____	_____
15 _____	_____	_____
16 _____	_____	_____
_____	_____	**TOTAL LIMIT & TOTAL AVAILABLE BALANCE**

MORE WAYS TO PAY OUR DEBT DOWN FASTER

1. **Work overtime or take on a part-time job**—This may be a foreign thought to some people, but we need to do whatever it takes to get money coming toward us instead of going away from us.

2. **Pray**—Now, I know that's really a foreign thought to some people, but we need to pray about our finances. "Lord, we need wisdom. We need Your guidance. We need doors to be opened for us and we need favor. Please direct our steps. Amen." We have not because we ask not.

   You want something but don't get it. You kill and covet, but you cannot have what you want. You quarrel and fight. You do not have, because you do not ask God.

   James 4:2 NIV

3. **Pay twice the minimum each month**—Because of the calculations credit card companies use to figure their minimum payments, if we'll just pay double that amount each month and not charge anything new, our cards will be paid off in roughly three years no matter what the balances are on them.

4. **Increase our abilities**—Remember II Kings 4:1. The man loved God and served God, but he still died broke. We don't get paid because we love Jesus.

   In Matthew 25, each servant got stuff according to his abilities. We're going to have to increase our abilities. We may need to go down to the local community college and take some classes. We may even need to develop a brand-new trade. If we improve ourselves, we'll be more valuable.

CREDIT HOUSE CLEANING

A good name is more desirable than great riches; to be esteemed is better than silver or gold.

Proverbs 22:1 NIV

A credit report is like a character reference in the world of money. It documents how we're managing our borrowing relationships and it's updated on a monthly basis. But because of human error, 42% of all credit reports contain mistakes. The only way to find out if there are mistakes on ours is to read what's in our files.

- We need to get copies of our credit reports from each of the three national credit bureaus. We need all three because they could all be different. *(See below for how to get them.)*

- We need to be sure we don't owe money somewhere and our credit is being ruined because we're not making payments on something we didn't know about. We may think we paid something off, but the lender may still show us as having an unpaid balance. (A divorce decree does not release us from legal responsibility on any account with our name on it.)

- Just because we pay off a debt doesn't mean our payment history will be removed. Any activity on an account or any judgments filed against us stay on our reports for seven years, except for Chapter 7 Bankruptcies, which stay on our reports for ten years.

- If we see something on our report which is incorrect, we should write the credit bureau immediately. (If we don't contact them, the mistake will stay on our file for years.)

CREDIT SCORING

Credit scoring is the numerical formula a lender uses to try to predict how risky it might be to lend us money.

Here's how it works: Once we fill out an application for a loan, the bank is going to enter that information into a computer. That is going to call up one of the major credit bureaus and they're going to put together a credit report right there on the spot. Then the lender is going to use that information to come up with what is called a "FICO score."

The number they give us on our FICO score is going to determine whether that lender will approve our loan or not. It will also determine the interest rate that lender offers us and any special payment terms or conditions he thinks he needs to put on our note.

Our FICO score takes into account information about our checking and savings accounts, our outstanding balances on any debts, our payment history, our salaries, how many loans and credit cards we've applied for, etc.

The better our credit history, the higher our FICO score is going to be. Scores range from 300 to 850. To be approved for a loan, we want our FICO score to be at least 650 or higher. To get the best interest rates and terms, over 750 is the ideal.

We can get all three *free* copies of our annual credit reports by visiting the website *www.annualcreditreport.com* or by calling 1-877-322-8228. For a fee, we can get our FICO scores directly from each credit bureau listed below.

Experian—National Consumer Assistance Center (formerly TRW)
www.experian.com   1-888-EXPERIAN (1-888-397-3742)

TransUnion—Consumer Relations Department
www.transunion.com   1-800-851-2574

Equifax—Consumer Affairs Department
www.equifax.com   1-800-685-1111

*(**Note: Watch the fine print** on websites offering a combined report from all three agencies. You'll note that **only one** of the reports is actually free through them and the other two will cost around $30. The **only place** you can order a combined report for **free** is at the website www.annualcreditreport.com or by calling 1-877-322-8228. As of this writing, several agencies are being investigated by the Federal Trade Commission for offering "free" reports tied to buying expensive services.)*

MONEY MISTAKES

Almost everyone who gets in financial trouble, puts themselves there in whole or in part. Here are some traps that will suck the life right out of our pocketbooks.

1. Co-Signing For Someone Else's Debt

He who puts up security for another will surely suffer, but whoever refuses to strike hands in pledge is safe.

Proverbs 11:15 NIV

2. Not Being Generous

It is possible to give away and become richer! It is also possible to hold on too tightly and lose everything. Yes, the liberal man shall be rich! By watering others, he waters himself.

Proverbs 11:24-25 TLB

If you give to the poor, your needs will be supplied! But a curse upon those who close their eyes to poverty.

Proverbs 28:27 TLB

3. Gambling

Wealth from gambling quickly disappears; wealth from hard work grows.
Proverbs 13:11 TLB

Don't play the lottery! (Americans spend more money each year on gambling than they do on groceries and four times as much money on lottery tickets than they do on tickets to the movies.)

4. **Falling For A Sales Pitch**

   Only a simpleton believes what he is told! A prudent man checks to see where he is going.

   Proverbs 14:15 TLB

   Don't buy anything unless you really need it. Don't pay full price for anything.

5. **Arrogance**

   True humility and respect for the Lord lead a man to riches, honor and long life.

   Proverbs 22:4 TLB

6. **Debt**

   Just as the rich rule the poor, so the borrower is servant to the lender.

   Proverbs 22:7 TLB

   Don't use credit cards for anything unless you have the cash to pay the full amount at the end of the month.

7. **Bribery**

   He who gains by oppressing the poor or by bribing the rich shall end in poverty.

   Proverbs 22:16 TLB

   Don't buy lavish gifts—especially for people you don't know or don't really like.

8. **Not Having A Spending Plan**

   Any enterprise is built by wise planning, becomes strong through common sense, and profits wonderfully by keeping abreast of the facts.

   Proverbs 24:3-4 TLB

9. **Getting Rich Quick And Greed**

   Trying to get rich quick is evil and leads to poverty. Greed causes fighting; trusting God leads to prosperity.

   Proverbs 28:22, 25 TLB

SIX STATEMENTS TO AVOID

Unfortunately, lots of people get taken in by what sounds like a really good deal from a slick salesman. If something sounds too good to be true, it usually is.

1. **"No money down!"** They don't say, "You'll just pay it on the tail end!"

2. **"No payments (and/or interest) for 12 months!"** They don't say they're accruing your interest during that time and you'll pay it eventually.

3. **"Buy now. Pay later."** They don't say, "You'll be paying interest later on that, too."

4. **"Bad credit? no credit? bankruptcy? No problem! We can put you in a new car today!"** Sure they can—at 24% interest!

5. **"Send no money!"** Nobody gives away stuff for free. If it's free, it's not worth anything.

6. **"Congratulations! You've won a free gift!"** Yeah right. Just what pumpkin wagon do you think I came in on?!

SEVEN BAD HABITS THAT WILL ROB YOU OF YOUR WEALTH

1. **Immorality**

   Keep to a path far from her, do not go near the door of her house, lest you give your best strength to others and your years to one who is cruel, lest strangers feast on your wealth and your toil enrich another man's house.

   Proverbs 5:10 NIV

2. **Getting Money Through Wickedness**

   The Lord will not let a good man starve to death, nor will he let the wicked man's riches continue forever.

   Proverbs 10:3 TLB

3. **Troubling Your Family**

   The fool who provokes his family to anger and resentment will finally have nothing worthwhile left. He shall be the servant of a wiser man.

   Proverbs 11:29 TLB

4. **Refusing Correction**

   If you refuse criticism you will end in poverty and disgrace; if you accept criticism you are on the road to fame.

   Proverbs 13:18 TLB

5. **Drunkenness And Gluttony**

   Don't carouse with drunkards and gluttons, for they are on their way to poverty. And remember that too much sleep clothes a man with rags.

   Proverbs 23:21 TLB

6. **Covering Your Sins**

   He who conceals his sins does not prosper, but whoever confesses and renounces them finds mercy.

   Proverbs 28:13 NIV

7. **Laziness!**

   But you—all you do is sleep. When will you wake up? "Let me sleep a little longer!" Sure, just a little more! And as you sleep, poverty creeps upon you like a robber and destroys you; want attacks you in full armor.

   Proverbs 6:9-11 TLB

   Hard work brings prosperity; playing around brings poverty.

   Proverbs 28:19 TLB

HOME OWNERSHIP

Owning a home is still the number-one American Dream. It's also still the best tax shelter available to the average working person.

I'm a real big believer in owning a home. My wife and I rented a place when we first got married. After a few years, though, we decided to build our own home. It stretched us and it took a while to get it done, but after we moved in, we realized it was one of the best financial decisions we had ever made.

It's Biblical to own property and a home. Let's look at what the Bible has to say about owning a home first. Then we'll look at some of the details on how to go about getting and keeping one.

HOME OWNERSHIP SCRIPTURES

Wicked men are overthrown and are no more, but the house of the righteous stands firm.

Proverbs 12:7 NIV

Every wise woman buildeth her house: but the foolish plucketh it down with her hands.

Proverbs 14:1

In the house of the righteous is much treasure: but in the revenues of the wicked is trouble.

Proverbs 15:6

House and riches are the inheritance of fathers and a prudent wife is from the LORD.

Proverbs 19:14

Finish your outdoor work and get your fields ready; after that, build your house.
Proverbs 24:27 NIV

And Jesus answered and said, Verily I say unto you, There is no man that hath left house, or brethren, or sisters, or father, or mother, or wife, or children, or lands, for my sake, and the gospel's, But he shall receive an hundredfold now in this time, houses, and brethren, and sisters, and mothers, and children, and lands, with persecutions; and in the world to come eternal life.

Mark 10:29-30

Except the LORD build the house, they labour in vain that build it: except the LORD keep the city, the watchman waketh but in vain.

Psalm 127:1

The LORD's curse is on the house of the wicked, but he blesses the home of the righteous.

Proverbs 3:33 NIV

There is treasure to be desired and oil in the dwelling of the wise; but a foolish man spendeth it up.

Proverbs 21:20

There shall no evil befall thee, neither shall any plague come nigh thy dwelling. For he shall give his angels charge over thee, to keep thee in all thy ways.
Psalm 91:10-11

HOW TO BUY A HOME

Here's the first thing we need to ask ourselves about home ownership:

"How much house can we afford?"

Here are three things our banker is going look at to answer that question. (Of course, we can figure these out by ourselves ahead of time, so we'll know what he's going to say we can borrow.)

1. The bank is going to tell us that we can only buy something that's two to three times our **annual income**. In other words, if we make $50,000 a year, our bank believes we could handle a $100,000 or a $150,000 mortgage.

2. The next thing our banker is going to do is review our **monthly income.** He's going to estimate that 28-33% of our monthly gross income can go to our mortgage payments. If we make $3,500 a month before taxes, he'll come up with $980 to $1,155 a month. (Some financial experts say if you want to have financial peace and build wealth, you should never buy a house with a mortgage that's more than 25% of your *take-home* pay.)

3. The third thing our banker is going to consider before he loans us any money is what kind of **debt load** we're carrying. (Remember our Debt-Payoff Chart? Our total debt is going to come into play whenever we're considering a loan.) The bank figures that about 36% of our monthly gross income is the maximum debt, including credit card payments, that we can comfortably handle. If we have a higher annual and monthly income, but our credit cards are all charged up to their limits, we're not going to qualify to buy the kind of house we really want.

    Something to note is that before we even look to find a house to buy, we should apply for a mortgage ahead of time. In order to "pre-qualify" us, our banker is going to look for proof of our current income (copies of our last tax returns and our recent pay stubs), information about our debt, the amount of cash we have, and our credit reports. We should get ourselves pre-approved before we go house shopping. Then we'll know what kind of house we should be looking for and what kind of deals we need to strike once we go out there to look.

The next question we need to ask ourselves before buying a house is:

"What kind of mortgage do we want?"

There are three main types of mortgages out there that we could consider. (Actually, there are more types of mortgages than we can shake a stick at, but most of them are all variations of these three—or they're too risky or too complicated to get involved with.)

1. **Fixed rate mortgages** are just what the name implies. They have a fixed rate of interest and our monthly principal payments will stay the same throughout the life of the loan. Popular choices are 15- or 30-year mortgages.

2. **Adjustable or variable-rate mortgages** have interest rates which change every year, every six months, or every quarter. These rates are determined by some financial index, such as the six-month U.S.

Treasury Bill rate or the Prime rate set by the Federal Reserve. We want to stay away from these loans, because if interest jumps up all of a sudden, our payments are going to jump, too.

3. **Two-step mortgages or "buy-downs"** are a good choice for new homeowners with low incomes and little money for a down payment. After five, seven, or a certain number of years, the payments on these loans increase, supposing that over time, our income will increase.

Once we find out what kind of mortgage we want, we need to ask:

"What about a down payment?"

There are two main things we need to consider when we're thinking about coming up with the earnest money on a home.

1. Most lenders expect us to have at least 10% of the purchase price in cash. Some will settle for as little as 3%. If we make a low down payment (under 20%), our lender is going to require that we pay for **private mortgage insurance.** This is a premium for an insurance policy we pay every month that protects the lender in case we quit paying our house payments. Private mortgage insurance (called "PMI") is going to cost us a lot more money in the long run.

   Once we have more than 20% equity in our homes, we need to call our lender to find out what their procedure is to take the PMI off and save ourselves $50 to $100 a month. (They won't send a notice when we've paid enough. They'll just keep charging us the PMI for the length of our loan, unless we contact them.)

2. Some **government mortgage programs** allow people to pay as little as 3% down. Some veterans may not have to make a down payment at all. Some first-time home buyers receive assistance with down payments and lower interest rates.

After we've got the down payment covered, the next thing we need to ask is:

"How much are the closing costs?"

This is what gets a lot of people who have never bought a home.

We can expect to pay around 5% to 7% of the purchase price of the home to cover attorney's fees, bank fees, land surveys, title insurance costs, taxes, mortgage-recording costs, etc. We need to ask the lender for a **"Good Faith Estimate,"** which will show the approximate amount of all these fees and what our payments are going to be once they tack on insurance, taxes and PMI. There are fees hidden in there we can't even imagine, so we need to be prepared. (Some government programs and some "motivated" sellers may provide assistance with closing costs.)

Next we can't forget to think about home improvements when we consider what kind of house we want to buy.

"How much will we need to maintain and improve our home once we've got it?"

The average homeowner spends around $2,500 a year in home improvements.

Some people think, "Well, my house is new. I'm not ever going to have to fix anything." But, trust me—there will be something unexpected they'll need to do, so they'd better get ready for it.

Later on, at some time in our lives, we're going to wonder if we still have the best deal on our mortgage or if there is something better out there. We'll ask:

"Should we refinance?"

The standard guideline is that if mortgage rates fall more than 2% below what our interest rate is, and if we're going to stay in our home for another three to five years, it's probably a good deal to refinance. Even when we refinance, closing costs can be at least 2% of the new loan, so we may still have to pay some money up front. (If the bank rolls the closing costs into the mortgage, we have to figure out whether it's worth it to add to the balance of the mortgage we have left.) There are tons of books and websites that offer refinancing calculation formulas to help us decide.

PAY OFF YOUR MORTGAGE QUICKER

If we have a 30-year mortgage, because of the "miracle" of compound interest, we're scheduled to pay our banker at least two or three times as much as the original purchase price of our home when it's all said and done. But we don't have to.

Let's say we put our house on a 15-year note instead. What's that going to do?

Number one, it's going to raise our payment. If we were going to borrow $150,000 on a 30-year note at 7% interest, instead of $999 a month, it would make our principal and interest payment $1,348 a month.

We may say, "That's an extra $349 a month. We're already scraping the bottom of the barrel to get by now."

Well, we'd better carefully consider what kind of house we want to buy then, because the flip-side of this is that if we put that house on the 30-year plan, at 7% interest, we would pay a total of $359,266 dollars over the life of our loan. If we put that home on a 15-year mortgage, we would only pay a total of $242,684 for the same house. That's a $116,582 savings! If we were to invest that money in the stock market or a mutual fund that gave us a 9% annual rate of return over 30 years, we'd be multimillionaires.

Let's take a look at the chart below.

A 30-Year Loan vs. A 15-Year Loan (7% Interest)

Cost	Years	Monthly Payment	Total Interest	Total Paid	Savings
$150,000	30	$999	$209,266	$359,266	$0
$150,000	15	$1,348	$92,684	$242,684	$116,582

Someone might say, "Well, I'm already in a 30-year mortgage. How am I going to fix that?

There are simple ways to pay off a mortgage early and save all that extra interest. For example, by paying an extra $100 a month toward the principal, we can shorten a 7%, $150,000, 30-year mortgage to 23 years. Or if we make just one extra payment each year, we can shorten that mortgage to just under 24 years. An extra $300 a month would reduce that 30-year mortgage down to 16 years.

REVERSE MORTGAGES

I want to mention this briefly for older people. There is such a thing called a "Reverse Mortgage." If you're a senior citizen and your home is paid for, I want you to be aware of something available to you. (I'm not saying you need to do this—but I'm telling you what's available if you have to use it.)

If you reach age 62 and don't have a sufficient monthly income to support yourself, you may qualify for a reverse mortgage where the money you've put into your house down through the years is loaned back to you.

Several government programs sponsored by HUD and Fannie Mae will appraise your house, determine its value, and arrange for a monthly payment to be deposited into your bank account in the same way that your Social Security check is automatically deposited for you. A reverse mortgage is not treated as income for tax purposes, so it won't put you into a higher tax bracket.

The only catch is that if your heirs want your house after you die, they will have to assume the responsibility for paying it off after they inherit your estate.

Some people may have worked all their lives, but they don't have a pension plan and they aren't drawing enough Social Security to make it financially. If you're in that situation, what a tremendous asset a reverse mortgage could be. You don't get to leave your kids a mortgage-free home, but it's better than having to starve to death. To some senior citizens, a reverse mortgage is a tremendous release from a life of poverty and financial disaster.

FIVE WAYS TO SAVE ON HOMEOWNER'S INSURANCE

Once we get into our homes, we ought to take a look at our homeowner's insurance policies and premiums and compare rates from several companies every year. Insurance rates typically rise about 10% to 20% annually. To avoid this, or to make sure we always have the best insurance possible at the lowest rates, there are five strategies we should use.

1. **Raise The Deductible**—Changing from a $500 to a $1,000 deductible can reduce our premiums by as much as 10% to 25%. If we're willing to bear the risk on small mishaps, our insurance company will reward us for it with lower premiums.

2. **Improve Our Home's Security Or Condition**—Dead bolts, smoke detectors and burglar alarms can reduce premiums by 5% to 15%. Another thing to consider is that due to fewer anticipated problems, buying a newer home can provide up to 10% to 15% savings on premiums.

3. **Ask For Discounts**—People who are retired, senior citizens, or people who work at home can probably get a 10% discount. Some business associations, alumni organizations and special groups can also get discounts on rates. We should find out if any of the associations we belong to offer such a benefit.

4. **Stay With One Company**—Longstanding policy holders normally get a 5% discount off annual premiums after two or three years. In addition, purchasing several policies (auto, homeowner's, life, etc.) from the same company provides leverage to negotiate a 5% to 10% discount on each.

5. **Stop Smoking**—Non-smokers save 10% to 15% on homeowner's insurance simply because their houses are less likely to burn down. Think about it!

CUT YOUR FOOD COSTS

A good wife watches for bargains.

Proverbs 31:18 TLB

The U.S. Department of Agriculture says that of the money parents spend on their kids, 15% to 20% goes for food. Let's look at some more statistics.

- In 2002, the average four-person household spent $6,693 on food per year.

- Affluent households (with gross incomes of $70,000 and up) spend an average of $8,874 on food per year.

- Since the year 1996, spending on take-out meals from restaurants has exceeded spending on meals consumed in those restaurants.

- Since 1997, spending on take-out meals from restaurants in America has exceeded spending on groceries each year.

- To capitalize on this, most supermarkets and grocery stores now offer more prepared food, such as what you find in a grocery store deli. Nearly 20% of all shoppers regularly buy whole meals at the supermarket. (Supermarket take-out food is a $100 billion business.)

SUPERMARKET SAVINGS TIPS

1. Plan menus for an entire week and always shop with a list.

2. Plan to make enough food for leftovers in order to save time and money. If you're going to take the time to cook, make your meals last two days instead of one.

3. Avoid impulse buying. Almost 50% of all grocery store purchases are unplanned (things that were not on our list).

4. Limit shopping time to half an hour. Studies show that customers spend approximately 50 cents a minute after spending a half hour in the store. (It's like being in a taxi-cab with the meter running. Get in and get out of there!)

5. Shop alone if at all possible. Spouses and children often cause us to compromise our lists.

6. Never shop when hungry. (We need to stop at the taco stand and get a 89¢ burrito before we walk into the supermarket or we'll want to buy everything in sight.)

7. Clip coupons. We can easily cut the grocery bill by as much as 10% to 20%. Some supermarkets double or even triple coupons on certain days, saving us even more. (Just don't use coupons to buy stuff that really isn't needed.)

8. Shop smart and check for off brands. Stores purposely stock their highest priced items at eye-level.

9. Always check unit prices. The price per pound or per ounce appears in tiny print on the shelf beneath each item. *(Believe it or not, I have a little fold-up magnifying glass I carry in my pocket so I can read those little numbers.)* Buying in bulk is not always cheaper.

10. Avoid food packaged in individual servings. Extra packaging boosts the product price.

11. Buy vegetables and fruits in their seasons when they're in abundant supply.

12. When buying meat, consider the amount of meat in the cut as well as the price per pound. Don't waste good money on a lot of bones and fat.

13. Serve main courses when they're on sale. If somebody in town is having a sale on chicken and it's 59¢ per pound, eat chicken for a week (roast chicken, chicken pot pie, fried chicken, barbecued chicken, chicken fricassee, chicken a la mode, etc.).

14. Avoid so-called convenience foods—especially the "designer" type. The illustration of "The Latté Factor™" by author David Bach in the book *Smart Couples Finish Rich* (New York, NY: Broadway Books, 2001) just blows my mind:

    Bach points out that the $10 a couple in their thirties spends each weekday on Starbucks lattés and muffins before they go to work adds up to more than $200 a month, or over $2,400 a year. Bach explains that if they decided to invest that money in a pre-tax retirement account earning 12% annually instead, by the time that couple retired at age 65, they would have a nest egg of just over $2.3 million dollars. *(To that I say, "God bless Folgers and Betty Crocker!")*

WHAT THE BIBLE SAYS ABOUT FOOD

I have been young, and now am old; yet have I not seen the righteous forsaken, nor his seed begging bread.

Psalm 37:25

And seek not ye what ye shall eat, or what ye shall drink, neither be ye of doubtful mind. For all these things do the nations of the world seek after: and your Father knoweth that ye have need of these things. But rather seek ye the kingdom of God; and all these things shall be added unto you.

Luke 12:29-31

Honour the LORD with thy substance, and with the firstfruits of all thine increase: So shall thy barns be filled with plenty, and thy presses shall burst out with new wine.

Proverbs 3:9-10

He that tilleth his land shall be satisfied with bread: but he that followeth vain persons is void of understanding.

Proverbs 12:11

He upholds the cause of the oppressed and gives food to the hungry. The LORD sets prisoners free.

Psalm 146:7 NIV

Do not love sleep or you will grow poor; stay awake and you will have food to spare.

Proverbs 20:13 NIV

And ye shall eat in plenty, and be satisfied, and praise the name of the LORD your God, that hath dealt wondrously with you: and my people shall never be ashamed.

Joel 2:26

THE BASICS ON INSURANCE
INSURANCE YOU PROBABLY NEED

A prudent person foresees the danger ahead and takes precautions; the simpleton goes blindly on and suffers the consequences.

Proverbs 22:3 NLT

1. **Life Insurance**—The only reason to buy life insurance is to meet our obligations to our family in the event of our death. Before we buy life insurance, we should ask ourselves this question: Who would starve or be homeless if we were to drop dead tomorrow? If the answer is no one, then we don't need life insurance.

- We should become familiar with the different types of policies available, such as whole life, term, etc. Term life insurance is usually a fraction of the cost of whole or universal life insurance. In most cases, term life is the best type of life insurance to buy. *(Don't let any slick salesman tell you that whole life insurance is a good investment. The purpose of insurance is to cover you against risk. There are much better ways to invest your hard-earned dollars than to sink them into the high commissions and low returns of a whole life policy.)*

- Cover a stay-at-home spouse. How much would we have to pay for child care to be able to work if our spouses were gone?

- Get coverage for as long as the kids will be around.

- Experts typically advise people to get a policy that is worth at least ten times their annual salary or more. If we make $50,000 a year, we probably need at least $500,000 of term life insurance.

- Single people with no dependents may need enough coverage to pay for funeral expenses.

2. **Health Insurance**—A full 50% of all bankruptcies in America are filed because of the inability to pay for medical expenses.

   - If we're insured by our employers, we should choose a PPO (a Preferred Provider Organization) over a regular major-medical policy to keep premiums down, if we have an option.

   - We need to read all our policy documents carefully and know what's included, what's excluded, and how to make a claim. We may need to ask a thousand questions and find a good friend or insurance agent who will help us go over all the fine print. We should never sign anything unless we know what everything means.

   - We should open a Flexible Spending Account (FSA) or a Health Savings Account (HSA), if that's an option.

   - If we provide our own insurance, as most people do, we can increase our co-payments and choose the highest deductibles we can handle. *(I found out that if I would carry a $5,000 deductible on my family policy, it cut the costs of my premiums in half.)* Insurance companies don't want to get stuck with all those little emergency room visits for stitches and such. If we're willing to pay more out of our pockets up front, almost anyone can afford to buy health insurance.

- The five leading causes of death in the United States are heart disease, diabetes, cancer, stroke from high blood pressure (hypertension), and AIDS. Note that each of these diseases is related to diet, exercise and lifestyle. For the most part, our health is in our own hands. Change our health. Save a lot of money.

3. **Auto Insurance**—Most states require that we have a certain amount of insurance to cover any damage we may do with our cars.

   - The average cost to insure a car has risen 44% in the last decade.

   - We don't want to buy coverage we don't need, but we do need to make sure our coverage includes bodily injury, liability, collision, comprehensive, uninsured motorist's coverage and property damage provisions.

   - We should buy a policy with a high liability limit and a high deductible.

4. **Homeowner's Or Renter's Insurance**—Refer to the information earlier in this section.

5. **Disability Insurance**—This type of insurance pays a certain percentage of our current income if an injury or illness renders us unable to work. Financial experts don't all agree whether this insurance is necessary for everyone or not. *(You're the best person to determine whether you need this type of coverage.)*

   - The risk level of our occupation and the elimination period we choose determines the cost of our premium. A high-wire walker, is going to pay higher rates than someone who makes donuts for a living.

   - A 180-day elimination period (the time that we'll have to wait before we draw any money) can cost a fraction of what a 30-day period costs us in premiums.

   - The amount of disability insurance we need to purchase should be based on our occupation and income.

INSURANCE YOU PROBABLY DON'T NEED

1. **Cancer insurance**—It usually duplicates coverage provided by health insurance.

2. **Accident insurance**—Ditto.

3. **Mortgage insurance**—It pays off our mortgage in the event of our death. Enough term life insurance would have the same benefit at about half the cost.

4. **Credit life insurance**—It pays off certain debts when we die and is usually bundled with a loan or a credit card. Enough term life coverage will do the same thing for less than 20% of the cost.

5. **Nursing home insurance**—Also known as long-term care insurance, it pays certain expenses our health insurance will not pay if we must enter a nursing home. *(Your personal situation may dictate that you should purchase this coverage, but the best plan is to build up your own assets to the point that they would be sufficient to cover the expense of nursing home care for you or one of your family members.)*

6. **Travel insurance**—Adequate life insurance provides the same coverage. *(Some credit card companies offer free travel insurance if you charge your travel arrangements on their cards.)*

7. **Extended warranties**—Most of these are filled with such stringent restrictions they aren't worth having.

OTHER WAYS TO SAVE MONEY
BUYING A USED CAR

Before we walk out on that car lot, we need to say this to ourselves over and over: "**Cars go down in value—monthly payments do not!**" People lose more money driving a new car off a lot than anything they'll ever put money into.

A friend of mine is a multimillionaire. He has a beautiful home and he's a very generous man who blesses his church and other ministries tremendously. But, he drives one of the nastiest cars I've ever been in.

I asked him one time, "How come you don't get yourself a decent car?"

He answered me with these two words: "**Bad math.**"

And you know, he's right. A car is only designed to get us from one place to another. We don't need to impress anybody. Because of depreciation, buying a car—whether it's new or used—is bad math. We need to think about that and not get all emotionally wrapped up in the process.

Here are four things we need to do when we have to buy a car.

1. **Research**—Consumer Reports' Annual Buying Guide lists cars in all price ranges which are rated as good buys over the last seven years. It also tells you which ones to avoid.

   The website www.edmunds.com also gives values and reliability ratings for used car models, dating as far back as twenty years. Some cars are classics, and some are lemons forever.

2. **Find a good source**—The Yellow Pages in a metro area are a good source for locating automobile auction houses and rental car companies who handle previously leased and former rental cars. (These kinds of cars are usually a great bargain and they have usually been well-maintained.) The internet also opens up a whole new world for car buyers who are willing to drive a few miles to save a few hundred bucks.

3. **Find a good mechanic or auto inspector**—We should have him examine the car we're interested in for a fee (usually under $150) to let us know if we're looking at a good deal or a lemon. (The website www.carfax.com can also provide us with the history of a used car's title for a relatively low fee.)

4. **Call the insurance company before buying**—Insurance companies use vehicle crash safety ratings to set the cost of collision and comprehensive coverage on automobiles. An insurance agent can help steer us to a safer make and model that may be much cheaper to insure. (The National Highway and Transportation Safety Agency also posts this info at www.nhtsa.gov.)

SAVE BIG AT THE BANK

The average cost of a checking account has risen more than 60% over the last five years, but the biggest expense incurred by people with checking accounts today is something that's totally within our control. It's paying fees for bounced checks. At $35 a pop, they really add up. Too many bounced checks can also damage a good credit rating, so we need to be extra careful to always monitor our balance.

Apart from that, one way we can save some dough is by switching from a bank to a credit union. If we paid more than $100 last year on bank fees (not counting fees for bounced checks), we need to find a credit union or—at the very least—a better bank for our checking account. Credit unions typically pay higher interest on savings accounts and usually have lower fees for their services because they're non-profit organizations. They usually offer the lowest interest rates on credit cards, too.

Another way we can save big is to order replacement checks from one of the following companies instead of from our bank. With them, people usually end up paying about the same amount for three or four boxes of checks that they would have paid if they had ordered them from the bank.

Checks Unlimited	1-800-299-0212	www.checksunlimited.com
Artistic Checks	1-800-243-2577	www.artisticcchecks.com
Designer Checks	1-800-859-7086	www.designerchecks.com

SAVE ON BIG-TICKET ITEMS

We can save a lot of money by purchasing items when they typically go on sale. Here's a list of when things are likely to be a good deal:

January	Appliances, bedding, books, linens, toys
February	Bedding, used cars, exercise equipment
March	Winter clothes
April	Spring clothing
May	Televisions
June	Summer clothes, electronics
July	Appliances, summer clothes
August	School supplies, furniture
September	New cars, dishes, cookware
October	School supplies
November	Winter clothes, used cars
December	Winter clothes

RETIREMENT PLANNING

Finishing is better than starting.

Ecclesiastes 7:8 NLT

Take a lesson from the ants, you lazybones. Learn from their ways and be wise! Even though they have no prince, governor, or ruler to make them work, they labor hard all summer, gathering food for the winter.

Proverbs 6:6-8 NLT

There are three major sources of retirement income. They are Social Security, pension plans, and personal savings and investments. Most companies are doing away with their pension plans, which means, if you don't have any money put back or invested, you're stuck with Social Security.

Without some major changes, the federal government says that by the year 2029, just as the last of the baby boomers turn 65, Social Security will only have 77% of the money it needs to pay benefits. When Social Security first started, there were 64 people paying money in for every one person who was drawing money out. Today, there are only three people paying money in for every one person drawing money out. The system appears to be in trouble. So we'd better not be relying on Social Security to get us through our golden years. (Even if we do get that check for $417 a month, we're going to have to develop a really cheap lifestyle.)

We need to be putting money back now in order to live a decent life after we retire. Unfortunately a lot of senior citizens today just can't make it on their Social Security benefits. They can't afford to retire—unless they decide not to eat.

Remember our statistics:

- The majority of Americans will retire with less than $10,000 in annual income.

- 85% of Americans, age 65 and older have less than $250 in savings.

Now, I have nothing against Wal-Mart or McDonald's, but I don't want to have to work when I'm 80. I don't want to die broke, leaving nothing behind for my children but debts. I don't want to have to move back in with my kids or have to accept government assistance. I want to be one of those four people the government tracks, who at age 65, is well off—or better yet—I want to be the one who is wealthy!

If we're going to retire with enough money for ourselves and have some left over for our children's children, we need to have an investment strategy.

There are volumes of books and articles which go into far more detail on planning for retirement than I can attempt to cover here. *(I've listed several in the resource section in the back of this book.)* But, I do want to lay out some basic questions that we need to answer when considering our goals for retirement and how we'll come up with a plan that will meet our individual needs:

1. **At what age do we plan to retire?** At age 55, 65 or 75?

2. **Will we be in good health?** Americans are living longer, but medical expenses and health care costs are on the rise. The federal government did a study recently which indicated that if people live to age 55 with no major health problems, it's a pretty good indicator that they'll probably live to age 85 without any. (They have a pattern established.) That's good news and that's bad news, because we'll live to a ripe old age, but we'll need more money to enjoy it.

3. **Will we travel?** If so, how often and to where?

4. **Will we have one house or two?** Can we afford the upkeep? Will we still have a mortgage?

5. **Will our children be out on their own?** Are we going to be raising our grandchildren?

6. **How long can we live on our own?** Where will we go when we can't, and how will we pay for it?

7. **After taxes, are our savings, investments, pension and Social Security positioned to outperform inflation?**

The answers we come up with on these basic questions will help us to lay the foundation for our plans for retirement. Of course, the earlier in life that we begin this planning, the better off we'll be in the long run. But even if we're approaching our golden years, it's never too late to set financial goals for ourselves and to take steps to reach them.

WILLS AND TRUSTS—YOUR ESTATE PLAN

> *A good man leaves an inheritance for his children's children, but a sinner's wealth is stored up for the righteous.*
>
>   *Proverbs 13:22 NIV*

> *If anyone does not provide for his relatives, and especially for his immediate family, he has denied the faith and is worse than an unbeliever.*
>
>   *I Timothy 5:8 NIV*

Seventy percent of all Americans do not have a valid will or trust. Yet dying without a proper estate plan can cost our families tens of thousands of dollars in legal fees and can potentially cause years of delay until our estates are settled.

Having an estate plan is scriptural. Did you know that Jesus left us a Last Will and Testament?

The Bible says that it's appointed unto every man once to die. Nobody wants to think about dying. But I've got news for you—it's not *IF* we're going to die—Darling, it's *WHEN* we're going to die. We know we're going to live a long time on the earth. God says so, but we all will go home eventually, if Jesus tarries. Once we get over that mental hump, planning for the future isn't as hard as it seems.

Here's what we'll need to start:

1. **The name of the person we want to choose to be the guardian of our minor children** in the event of our death.

2. **A list of whom we want to receive our assets** upon our death and how we want the assets to be transferred to them.

3. **The current value of our estate.** (Remember our net worth worksheet.)

The next thing we need to do is find a good estate planning attorney and we need to arm ourselves with some basic information.

Here are three terms we should be familiar with:

1. **Last Will And Testament**—A will is a legal document that directs where we want our assets to go after our death. (A person who dies without a will is said to have died "intestate." That means that state law will determine who receives their assets, and a state judge will determine who becomes the guardian of any minor children.)

   At the very least, every adult needs a will.

2. **Probate**—If we left a will, probate is a court procedure in which a judge in the state where we died has to authenticate that will and make sure that it is valid. (Even though we may have had a will, the title to our property will not automatically transfer to our designated beneficiary without first going through court, which is a lengthy and costly process.) Our designated heirs could lose nearly everything we leave if our will gets tied up in probate, becomes subject to fees and estate taxes, or is challenged.

   First, the state will require a public advertisement of the probate process on our estate and notice will be given to all potential creditors who have an interest to come forward. (This is the stage where forgotten relatives may show up on the scene to demand their "fair share.")

If we didn't have a will or a trust, probate is the process in which a state judge is going to decide who gets our stuff and who raises our kids.

3. **Revocable Living Trust**—Usually called a "trust," it involves the process of creating a legal entity similar to a corporation which contains our assets. Probate laws do not apply to assets owned by a trust. Once the trust is formed, funding occurs when we transfer ownership of our property into the name of the trust.

    Having a trust means that when we die, our family can enjoy immediate access to our assets without going through probate and without the public knowing about it.

    Another advantage of a trust *(and there are more types of trusts than just the type I mentioned here)* is that they can be a part of a strategy to reduce estate taxes. The cost for a living trust can range anywhere from $500 to as much as $5,000, however, estate taxes can run as high as 55% of an estate's value. A trust can be a very smart investment, if we plan on having significant assets.

FIVE STEPS TO A GOOD NIGHT'S SLEEP

The last thing I want to cover in this section is the five steps we can take that will help us to lay our heads down on our pillows each night and not be tormented by fear concerning our finances. Each of these steps builds on the one before it and will take time to accomplish, but in the end, the confidence these steps will give us is well worth the effort.

1. **We need to start putting back money until we have enough to cover at least three months' worth of our expenses.** According to Money Magazine, 75% of all families will have a major financial setback in any ten-year period.

    Now don't panic! We don't have to do this overnight. We can start by building up $1,000 or $2,000 as an emergency fund. Once we're at that mark, we need to keep faithfully tucking money away until we have enough to pay our house payment, buy groceries, put gas in the car, and pay our insurance for three months. *It can be done—and the Lord will help us.* (If we're like most people, we're already spending $1,000 in take out drinks and snacks each year anyway.)

2. **We need to begin working toward paying off all our debt.** *We can do it!* People do it everyday. People who don't know Jesus do it everyday.

We start by paying down all our credit cards and unsecured debts and when they're gone, we work on paying off our car(s) and house early. (If we've learned to be good stewards with our spending, we'll hardly even miss that extra $100 a month.)

3. **We ought to invest at least 10% to 15% of our gross household income in a tax-free or tax-deferred retirement plan.** If we're only middle-income earners, we're already saving the equivalent of at least 28% by putting pre-tax dollars into a plan. Depending on our tax bracket, we might be saving 35% or more in taxes alone. That's not even counting whatever interest rate we're making on our investments. If our employer will match any of our retirement dollars, this is really a no-brainer.

4. **If we have kids, we're going to need to save for their college.** College graduates earn 80% to 90% more than people without a degree. *(See Section Three.)*

5. **We need to build our wealth.** The whole purpose of riches is to use our money to benefit others. If we'll keep our focus right, God will bless us so we can be a blessing to our families, our churches, our communities and beyond.

$ection 3

channels
of income

Gifts, Callings,
Vocations And Work

channels
of income

GIFTS, CALLINGS, VOCATIONS AND WORK

WHAT WE NEED:

God designs for each of us to have a vocation—an occupation—a job.

WHY WE NEED IT:

We are responsible to provide for ourselves and for our families.

HOW DO WE FIND WHAT GOD WANTS US TO DO?

- Everyone is gifted by God with some unique ability.

- We must find out what our gifts are and begin to steward them.

- To increase our income, we must increase our abilities and develop a strong work ethic.

We get paid for two things on this earth. We get paid for what we know and for what we do. If we don't know more than anyone else, or we can't do more than anyone else, we won't get paid more than anyone else. Our first task in the area of our vocation is to find out what unique abilities God has gifted us with and begin to steward those gifts to their fullest potential.

FINDING OUR GIFTS

If God's Word says we're responsible to provide for our families, we need to know what we're good at because we're going to get paid for that. We need to find out what our gifts and callings are, and we've got to learn how to turn our God-given talents into provision for our households.

What God gives us is just in raw form. We've got to do our part and be good stewards of our abilities, if we're going to turn them into cash. That means, we're going to have to develop a strong work ethic.

Work is not a bad word. It's a blessing. I've had times when I've worked and times when I haven't. Trust me, Friend, working is better.

When I was born nobody told me what my gift was. They gave my mother a box of cloth diapers and a binky. They didn't tell my mom, "...And by the way, here's God's plan for your son's life, Mrs. McGee."

No, the Bible says, eye hasn't seen the plan God has for me. Ear hasn't heard it, and it hasn't entered into the heart of man the things that God has prepared for me. But by His spirit, God has revealed it (I Corinthians 2:9-10).

In other words, I've got to ask God what His plan for me is.

Every person needs to have a vision for what God wants them to do in life. Without a vision, we'll perish (Proverbs 29:18).

> *And the LORD answered me, and said, Write the vision, and make it plain upon tables, that he may run that readeth it. For the vision is yet for an appointed time, but at the end it shall speak, and not lie: though it tarry, wait for it; because it will surely come, it will not tarry.*
>
> *Habakkuk 2:2-3*

God told Habakkuk, "I've got a vision, but it's not coming tomorrow. It's not coming next week, next month or next year, but it is coming. But if you don't write it down you're going to forget about it."

We should be asking God what it is He has for us, and when we find out, we need to write it down. The next part is believing, confessing, praying and working to bring it to pass.

> *Even while we were still there with you we gave you this rule: "He who does not work shall not eat." Yet we hear that some of you are living in laziness, refusing to work, and wasting your time gossiping. In the name of the Lord Jesus Christ we appeal to such people—we command them—to quiet down, get*

to work, and earn their own living.

II Thessalonians 3:10-12 TLB

Blessed is the man that walketh not in the counsel of the ungodly, nor standeth in the way of sinners, nor sitteth in the seat of the scornful. But his delight is in the law of the LORD; and in his law doth he meditate day and night. And he shall be like a tree planted by the rivers of water, that bringeth forth his fruit in his season; his leaf also shall not wither; and whatsoever he doeth shall prosper.

Psalm 1:1-3

He that walketh with wise men shall be wise: but a companion of fools shall be destroyed.

Proverbs 13:20

What are these passages saying?

We'd better watch who we hang out with. We want to go somewhere in life. We want to make our mark for God. We want to be able to provide for our families more than adequately. To do that, we'd better watch who we run with. We'd better not be hanging out with sinners, listening to the ungodly or sitting with people who gripe all the time. We'd better get a vision for our lives and get busy doing it. *(People with a vision would like to gripe; they just don't have time.)*

So how do we find a vision for our lives?

We find out what our God-given gifts are and then go to work.

AN EXAMPLE FROM HISTORY

At age 19, Joseph Pulitzer came to America from Hungary. He didn't speak any English but he made his way to St. Louis and got a job at a German-language newspaper. He saved what he could from his small salary and within five years, he had taught himself English and bought a newspaper that was on the brink of bankruptcy. Within a year, the circulation of his paper had doubled. Pulitzer sold the paper at a huge profit and moved to New York. There he bought the New York World newspaper. The World became most popular paper in America, generating an annual ad revenue of over $2 million. When Pulitzer died in 1911, his estate was valued at well over $25 million, part of which was designated to create the "Pulitzer Prize" for outstanding journalism.

There was a man who came to America with no education, who couldn't even speak English, but through hard work and diligence, found out what he was gifted at, and he got after it.

Every one of us is born with a gift. We all have an ability—a grace gift from God. We have to be diligent to recognize what it is and we've got to get busy.

"THIS IS MY LIFE" NOTEBOOK

One of the simplest things I did to help the kids in the Christian school I directed find out what God was calling them to do was to put together a notebook for each of the students. I bought three-ring binders at Wal-Mart and put eight pages in each one of them. On the cover of each notebook, I inserted a page that said, "This Is My Life" *(Figure 1)*.

I also made books like this for all of my kids and I made one for myself and for my wife, too. It's amazing how a simple notebook like this can help define what it is that God has called us to do and help us to establish a plan for the future. To make one for each of your family members, follow the instructions in this section.

The first page that needs to go inside this notebook is a page with your name on it *(Figure 2)*. You need to go to the library or go online and do some research on your name.

What does your name mean?

I know your mother might have named you after your grandfather, your grandmother, or your aunt or uncle, but God said He knew your name even before your mom and dad did. Names are prophetic. They mean something.

> *A good name is rather to be chosen than great riches....*
>
> *Proverbs 22:1*

Make your name a name of honor.

The next six pages in the notebook have personalized scriptures on them. Each one has its own page *(Figures 3-8)*.

Page two of my notebook says this:

"Joe, all the days ordained for you were recorded in God's book before a single day had passed."

> *You saw me before I was born. Every day of my life was recorded in your book. Every moment was laid out before a single day had passed.*
>
> *Psalm 139:16 NLT*

Don't you love that?

God had a book with my name in it before I was ever conceived. Before there was a planet for me to stand on, God saw me coming. God looked down through time and saw the future. God sees me two days from now, two weeks from now, two months from now and two years from now. God will order my steps, direct my paths and show me things to come.

Why?

Because He's seen tomorrow.

Page three in my book says:

"Joe, before I formed you in the womb, I knew you. Before you were born, I set you apart..."

> *Before I formed you in the womb I knew [and] approved of you [as My chosen instrument], and before you were born I separated and set you apart, consecrating you; [and] I appointed you as a prophet to the nations.*
> *Jeremiah 1:5 AMP*

Page four adds Jeremiah 29:11 to my book. It says:

"Joe, I know the plans I have for you, declares the Lord, plans to prosper you, not to harm you, plans to give you a future and a hope."

> *"For I know the plans I have for you," says the LORD. "They are plans for good and not for disaster, to give you a future and a hope."*
> *Jeremiah 29:11 NLT*

God's got a great plan for my life. It's not based on me. God looked down through time, saw every sin I ever committed, every lie I'd ever tell, every nasty thing I'd ever do, and still said, "Joe, you're worth my Son to me. I have a great plan for your life."

The whole purpose of this notebook is to plant a vision for your life. Before you go out to earn money, you need to find out what you're going to earn money with.

What are you earning money for?

What are you doing here on this planet?

You were born for a reason. You weren't just an accident. I don't care how you were conceived. God Almighty saw you coming. You may have had a father of your flesh who didn't expect you, want you, provide for you or love you, but you have a Father of your spirit who did expect you. You didn't catch Him by surprise. He loves you. He's going to provide for you. He has a divine plan for your life.

How do I know that?

I know it by His Word.

Jeremiah 33:3 is the scripture written on the next page of my notebook. Here it is with my name:

"Joe, call unto me, and I will answer you, and show you great and mighty things, which you know not."

> *'Call to me and I will answer you. I'll tell you marvelous and wondrous things that you could never figure out on your own.'*
>
> *Jeremiah 33:3 MSG*

God has no small plans for anybody. He's got great and mighty plans for everybody.

On page six in my book, I've written Romans 11:29 from the Living Bible.

"Joe, God's gifts and His call on your life are irrevocable. He will never withdraw them."

> *For God's gifts and his call can never be withdrawn; he will never go back on his promises.*
>
> *Romans 11:29 TLB*

God's plan for our lives is not based on us—the IQ we have, the gifts we possess or our talent. We didn't earn it. We didn't deserve it. We didn't ask for it. We didn't pray for it. It is a grace gift given to us by God. His plan is a great plan. It has a future. It has prosperity. It's got hope. We cannot sin bad enough to make Him erase it (Romans 11:29).

But God won't make us live His plan. That's why He said *"...I set before you life and death, blessing and cursing: you choose..."* (Deuteronomy 30:19). Every day we get to *choose* to serve God.

God gives gifts to every human on this planet. There are people gifted to make millions of dollars on Wall Street, yet they may not know or serve God. Many people are gifted as athletes, musicians, entertainers, inventors, scientists, doctors, lawyers and business people. Everybody is good at something.

Where do you think they got those gifts?

They got them from God.

God gives us the freedom to choose. People can serve God. They can serve the devil. They can use their gifts, or not—steward them or not. Once God gives a gift, it's irrevocable. God will not take it back!

Even the devil was gifted by God. Ezekiel 28 says that Lucifer was gifted in four areas. *(Read it for yourself.)* Lucifer was full of wisdom, perfect in beauty, in charge of the wealth and in charge of the music of Heaven. Those were the things God gifted him to do. When he got fired from his job and got kicked out of Heaven like a lightning bolt, he didn't lose his gifts.

He still knows about wisdom, except now it's perverted. So now he's crafty. It's a different kind of wisdom. If he can't make you arrogant about being smart, he'll make you a smart alec.

Beauty! He makes beauty a multi-billion-dollar industry. You've got too much flesh, we'll suck some out. You don't have enough? We'll shove some in. You don't like your nose? We can get you a new one, you know. The devil's got people messing with their flesh. Every shopping center in America has an aerobic center and a tanning salon. Why? Nobody likes the way they look.

Lucifer was in charge of music—every kind of music. He uses music as a tool, because you remember what you sing. That's why we teach our children their ABCs by singing to them. God knew that—except we were supposed to be singing His Word—psalms, hymns and spiritual songs, making melody in our hearts to the Lord. Instead we're singing, "Take this job and shove it!" or "Born to lose." We weren't meant to be singing that.

Satan was also in charge of the wealth, and certainly, we've made money a god. We were supposed to be in charge of money. We were created to handle God's wealth. But what happens when we don't know God's Word? We make the Creation our god instead of the Creator.

On page seven of my notebook, it says this:

"Joe, use the gift you have received, and serve others faithfully, administering God's grace in various forms."

> *Each one should use whatever gift he has received to serve others, faithfully administering God's grace in its various forms.*
> *I Peter 4:10 NIV*

In other words, I not only have a call on my life, I have been divinely gifted to fulfill that call. I might not have ever walked it out. Maybe I've walked in darkness all my life. That's why it's so important that we have preachers and teachers and moms and dads and pastors and mentors, because we need to hear the Word.

Nobody's born knowing what they're supposed to do—**everybody's born an airhead!** It takes God, and revelation from men and women of God, to bring out God's plan. But everybody's been gifted to do something on this planet.

The last pages of my notebook have a sample list of vocations for me, using my gifts *(Figure 9)*, and a copy of a test found in the book called *Discovering Your God-Given Gifts* by Don and Katie Fortune (Grand Rapids, MI: Chosen Books, 1987).

The Fortunes have designed a series of tests based on Romans 12:6-9. There's a test for adults and one for kids. There's one for junior-high-aged children and one for senior-high-aged kids. They've even got a book for married couples called *Understanding Each Other's Gifts.*

Why are you the way you are?

You were "bent" or gifted that way.

Are you a prophetically motivated individual? A perceiver? Black and white? Right and wrong? Yes or no? Not much compassion or gray area?

Are you an exhorter?

Are you a teacher?

Are you compassionate?

Are you a giver?

Everybody's born with gifts and "bents" to serve our brothers and sisters in the Body of Christ. But those gifts don't stop working when we walk outside the church. Those are the very same gifts we're going to earn a living with.

The results of the test will tell you that somebody with your likes and dislikes and your gifts and abilities would probably do well in one of the vocations which are listed. It's not "thus saith the Lord" that you have to do it, but somebody with your gifts and abilities would do well in one of these careers.

For example, when I took the test—and I take it every year with my family at vacation time—this is my list of possible vocations based on my gifts. It says I would do well as an advertising executive or an auctioneer. I can't tell you how many people have said that to me. "Joe, slow down! Please slow down." When they transcribe my teaching tapes, they say that most people end up with about thirty pages of material when a forty-five-minute teaching tape is transcribed, but my messages usually come out to around sixty or seventy pages! I'd be a great as an auctioneer!

My test results also say I'd be good as a business owner, a contractor, an evangelist, an investment fund manager, a landscaper, a minister, a missionary, an occupational therapist, a paramedic, a realtor, a recreation director, a retailer, a sales person, a social worker, a sociologist, a teacher or a travel agent.

You know, in my life, I've done many of those things already.

Isn't that a shame, that someone can be a believer all their life, and never know what they're gifted to do?

That's not God's plan. We need to find out what we're good at. Even the people who work at the unemployment center are able to help pinpoint what someone is gifted at. We're going to make money with our strengths.

Now that doesn't mean we can let our weaknesses flail in the wind.

No, it's said that there are three parts to every person's job. One third of a job is usually the part that we're good at—the part we really like doing. When we do that part of our job we usually get a lot of praise. But then there's usually another third of our job that we *can* do—that is, we'll do it if somebody puts enough pressure on us, but it's not the best part of what we do. Finally, there's that last third of our job that we just don't like doing at all. We usually hate that part. When we do it, it's the part that we're more likely to get criticized for. If we don't develop a good work ethic, we'll avoid that part of our job like the plague. We'll put off doing it forever.

It's funny, but how successful we become in life will usually depend on how much time we put into that third part we're not good at. We have to shore up the areas where we're weak, not just confine ourselves to the areas where we're the strongest. We can't let our weaknesses destroy us. We have to be diligent and improve ourselves all around.

So what is it going to take for us to be successful?

First of all, we have to find out what we're gifted at. We can take some tests and do some research and we're going to have to pray and ask God what He wants us to do. Then we need to develop our gifts and our work ethic and be diligent.

The next few pages show what my "This Is My Life" notebook looks like. I encourage you to make one for yourself.

(Figure 1)

THIS IS MY LIFE

Joe Alan McGee

(Figure 2)

Joe (Hebrew)

God will add; wise and understanding

Uniting to bring about increase or improvement; possessing inside information; marked by keen and unusual discernment when dealing with people and situations; having a capacity for sound judgment; able to teach, advise and persuade; having the power to make experiences intelligible by applying concepts and categories

Alan (Irish)

Harmonious, handsome

Marked by agreement and balanced interrelationships with spontaneous impulse; able to make all parts agreeably related; having a pleasing and dignified appearance; marked by skill, cleverness, graciousness and generosity

Joe Alan McGee

A man able to bring about increase and improvement in people and situations, teaching and persuading with spontaneous impulse, bringing agreement and balance to relationships, having the power to make experiences intelligible by applying concepts and categories, marked by his skill, cleverness, graciousness and generosity

A good name is rather to be chosen than great riches....
Proverbs 22:1

(Figure 3)

Joe Alan McGee,

all the days ordained for you were recorded in God's book before a single day had passed.

You saw me before I was born. Every day of my life was recorded in your book. Every moment was laid out before a single day had passed.

                                        Psalm 139:16 NLT

(Figure 4)

Joe Alan McGee,

before I formed you in the womb, I knew you. Before you were born, I set you apart...

Before I formed you in the womb I knew [and] approved of you [as My chosen instrument], and before you were born I separated and set you apart, consecrating you; [and] I appointed you as a prophet to the nations.
                              Jeremiah 1:5 AMP

(Figure 5)

Joe Alan McGee,

I know the plans I have for you, declares the Lord, plans to prosper you, not to harm you, plans to give you a future and a hope.

"For I know the plans I have for you," says the LORD.
"They are plans for good and not for disaster, to give you
a future and a hope."

Jeremiah 29:11 NLT

(Figure 6)

Joe Alan McGee,

call unto me, and I will answer you, and show you great and mighty things, which you know not.

'Call to me and I will answer you. I'll tell you marvelous and wondrous things that you could never figure out on your own.'

Jeremiah 33:3 MSG

(Figure 7)

Joe Alan McGee,

God's gifts and His call on your life are irrevocable. He will never withdraw them.

For God's gifts and his call can never be withdrawn; he will never go back on his promises.

                                        Romans 11:29 TLB

(Figure 8)

Joe Alan McGee,

use the gift you have received, and serve others faithfully, administering God's grace in various forms.

Each one should use whatever gift he has received to serve others, faithfully administering God's grace in its various forms.

I Peter 4:10 NIV

(Figure 9)

JOE'S GOD-GIVEN GIFTS:

Administrator, Exhorter, Teacher, Giver

FIRST LIST

Advertising Executive
Ambassador
Auctioneer
Guidance Counselor
Minister
Personnel Manager
Public Relations Director
Recreation Director
Religious Education Director
Writer

SECONDARY LIST

Business Owner
City Planner
Contractor
Department Store Manager
Evangelist
Hospital Administrator
Hotel Manager
Investment Fund Manager
Journalist
Landscaper
Military Officer
Missionary
Occupational Therapist
Paramedic
Politician
Radio/TV Announcer
Realtor
Social Worker
Travel Agent

FAMOUS FAILURES

It's easy to look at successful people and assume that they get all the breaks in life and never fail at anything, but nothing could be farther from the truth.

Albert Einstein   He was four years old before he could speak.

Thomas Edison   His teachers told him he was too stupid to learn anything.

Walt Disney   He was fired by an editor who claimed he didn't have any good ideas.

Enrico Caruso   His music teacher once told him, "You have no voice at all."

Abraham Lincoln   He entered the Black Hawk War as a captain and came out as a private, had two businesses fail, suffered a nervous breakdown, and was defeated in seven different elections before he was elected President of the United States.

Alexander Graham Bell   He was laughed at most of his life as he tried to raise money to produce his invention the telephone.

What do these great men have in common?

They all failed, but they kept on trying until they were successful. We can't assume we're going to hit a home run the first time we go to the plate. It's going to take some practice and some time, but if we're diligent we will get there.

Let's look at what the Word says about being diligent.

> *And whatsoever ye do, do it heartily, as to the Lord, and not unto men.*
> *Colossians 3:23*

> *Whatsoever thy hand findeth to do, do it with thy might; for there is no work, nor device, nor knowledge, nor wisdom, in the grave, whither thou goest.*
> *Ecclesiastes 9:10*

> *Keep thy heart with all diligence; for out of it are the issues of life.*
> *Proverbs 4:23*

> *He becometh poor that dealeth with a slack hand: but the hand of the diligent maketh rich.*
> *Proverbs 10:4*

The hand of the diligent shall bear rule: but the slothful shall be under tribute.

Proverbs 12:24

The soul of the sluggard desireth, and hath nothing: but the soul of the diligent shall be made fat.

Proverbs 13:4

The thoughts of the diligent tend only to plenteousness; but of every one that is hasty only to want.

Proverbs 21:5

Seest thou a man diligent in his business? he shall stand before kings; he shall not stand before mean men.

Proverbs 22:29

For a just man falleth seven times, and riseth up again: but the wicked shall fall into mischief.

Proverbs 24:16

Whatever we're called and gifted to do, on the way there we're going to fall on our faces a thousand times. The Bible says the righteous fall seven times a day and then we get back up. We're not known as the perfect people. We're known as the "getting-back-up people." We can get back up with God's power and fulfill His plan.

I can do all things through Christ which strengtheneth me.

Philippians 4:13

I thank my God always on your behalf, for the grace of God which is given you by Jesus Christ; That in every thing ye are enriched by him, in all utterance, and in all knowledge; Even as the testimony of Christ was confirmed in you: So that ye come behind in no gift; waiting for the coming of our Lord Jesus Christ.

I Corinthians 1:4-7

That the God of our Lord Jesus Christ, the Father of glory, may give unto you the spirit of wisdom and revelation in the knowledge of him: The eyes of your understanding being enlightened; that ye may know what is the hope of his calling, and what the riches of the glory of his inheritance in the saints, And what is the exceeding greatness of his power to us-ward who believe, according to the working of his mighty power.

Ephesians 1:17-19

Blessed be the LORD my strength, which teacheth my hands to war, and my fingers to fight.

Psalm 144:1

Abide in me, and I in you. As the branch cannot bear fruit of itself, except it abide in the vine; no more can ye, except ye abide in me. I am the vine, ye are the branches: He that abideth in me, and I in him, the same bringeth forth much fruit: for without me ye can do nothing.

John 15:4-5

If ye abide in me, and my words abide in you, ye shall ask what ye will, and it shall be done unto you.

John 15:7

For by thee I have run through a troop; and by my God have I leaped over a wall.

Psalm 18:29

Nay, in all these things we are more than conquerors through him that loved us.
Romans 8:37

But my God shall supply all your need according to his riches in glory by Christ Jesus.

Philippians 4:19

Do you know what Jesus told us to pray for in the Last Days?

He didn't tell us to pray for miracles, signs and wonders, the downpouring, the outflowing, the river, the fire, the wind, or the rain.

Do you know what He said we would need to pray for?

Workers! (Matthew 9:38)

According to Jesus, we're going to have a shortage of labor. People will not want to work in the Last Days. So if we'll be diligent and rely on God's ability, we'll be surprised at how successful we can become.

GOD USES US RIGHT WHERE WE ARE

John Mason wrote a book called *An Enemy Called Average* (Tulsa, OK: Insight Publishing Group, 1990). He says we don't need to do anything else for God to use us than to begin to do what we know to do right now. It's that simple. We just need to start doing what we know. Throughout the Bible, God used many people from all backgrounds and experiences to fulfill His plans on earth.

Abraham, a wanderer, became a friend of God and the father of many nations.

Moses, a stutterer, became a mighty deliverer.

Deborah, a housewife, became a Judge of God's people.

Esther, an orphan, became a beautiful queen.

David, a shepherd boy, became a mighty king.

Mary, an unknown virgin, gave birth to the Son of God.

Paul, the great persecutor of the Church, became the greatest missionary in history and the author of two-thirds of the New Testament.

We may not be successful the first time out. We may not get the best salary right out of school. But if we'll be diligent, and use the abilities and gifts God has given us, He'll watch over that. As long as we're good stewards, He will increase what we put our hands to.

GOD'S WORD ON WORK

Now here is a command, dear brothers, given in the name of our Lord Jesus Christ by his authority: Stay away from any Christian who spends his days in laziness and does not follow the ideal of hard work we set up for you. For you well know that you ought to follow our example: you never saw us loafing; we never accepted food from anyone without buying it; we worked hard day and night for the money we needed to live on, in order that we would not be a burden to any of you. It wasn't that we didn't have the right to ask you to feed us, but we wanted to show you, firsthand, how you should work for your living. Even while we were still there with you, we gave you this rule: "He who does not work shall not eat." Yet we hear that some of you are living in laziness, refusing to work, and wasting your time in gossiping. In the name of the Lord Jesus Christ we appeal to such people—we command them—to quiet down, get to work, and earn their own living.

II Thessalonians 3:6-15 TLB

May the favor of the Lord our God rest upon us; establish the work of our hands for us—yes, establish the work of our hands.

Psalm 90:17 NIV

Man goeth forth unto his work and to his labour until the evening.

Psalm 104:23

It's normal to get up and go to work every day.

He also that is slothful in his work is brother to him that is a great waster.

Proverbs 18:9

Even a child is known by his doings, whether his work be pure, and whether it be right.

Proverbs 20:11

Finish your outdoor work and get your fields ready; after that, build your house.

Proverbs 24:27 NIV

For if any be a hearer of the word, and not a doer, he is like unto a man beholding his natural face in a glass: For he beholdeth himself, and goeth his way, and straightway forgetteth what manner of man he was. But whoso looketh into the perfect law of liberty, and continueth therein, he being not a forgetful hearer, but a doer of the work, this man shall be blessed in his deed.

James 1:23-25

The desire of the slothful killeth him; for his hands refuse to labour.

Proverbs 21:25

I went by the field of the slothful, and by the vineyard of the man void of understanding; And, lo, it was all grown over with thorns, and nettles had covered the face thereof, and the stone wall thereof was broken down. Then I saw, and considered it well: I looked upon it, and received instruction. Yet a little sleep, a little slumber, a little folding of the hands to sleep: So shall thy poverty come as one that travelleth; and thy want as an armed man.

Proverbs 24:30-34

Diligent hands will rule, but laziness ends in slave labor.

Proverbs 12:24

The slothful man roasteth not that which he took in hunting: but the substance of a diligent man is precious.

Proverbs 12:27

The way of the slothful man is as an hedge of thorns: but the way of the righteous is made plain.

Proverbs 15:19

The slothful man saith, There is a lion without, I shall be slain in the streets.

Proverbs 22:13

As a door turns on its hinges, so a sluggard turns on his bed. The sluggard buries his hand in the dish; he is too lazy to bring it back to his mouth. The sluggard is wiser in his own eyes than seven men who answer discreetly.

Proverbs 26:14-16 NIV

Lazy hands make a man poor, but diligent hands bring wealth.

Proverbs 10:4 NIV

Lazy people want much but get little, but those who work hard will prosper and be satisfied.

Proverbs 13:4 NLT

She looketh well to the ways of her household, and eateth not the bread of idleness. Her children arise up, and call her blessed; her husband also, and he praiseth her. Many daughters have done virtuously, but thou excellest them all. Favour is deceitful, and beauty is vain: but a woman that feareth the LORD, she shall be praised. Give her of the fruit of her hands; and let her own works praise her in the gates.

Proverbs 31:27-31

For as the body without the spirit is dead, so faith without works is dead also.

James 2:26

WORKING TODAY

We're going to have to work. We have to find out what we're called and gifted to do and get busy using our gifts.

I can imagine the wheels turning as people are reading this. "Oh, it's tough out there, Joe. It's different than it was ten or twenty years ago."

Certainly it is!

I was born in 1951. I've seen the workplace change. I've worked at three different secular companies. I've worked for two different churches. I've been on my own for over a dozen years in my own ministry.

I want you to know that I don't have my head stuck in a barrel. I understand that things have changed in the workplace, but God has not changed. He is still our Provider. He understands what's going on in this world, but He has given us a way to prosper, even in the midst of a perverse and wicked generation— even in the midst of an unstable economy. If we'll follow His plan, we won't just survive, we will thrive.

According to *The Future Of Success* (New York, NY: Vintage Books, 2000), by Robert Reich, the former U.S. Secretary of Labor, things have changed tremendously in the American workplace in the last several decades. *(When I read this book and saw the many new trends in the workplace that the author highlighted, it was an eye opener.)*

Reich says, that the deepest concern of America right now is the fragmenting of our communities and the challenge of keeping our own integrity in tact.

That's what God warned us about when He said, "In the Last Days perilous times will come." He was telling us that something about the integrity of men in these End Times would go haywire, He said, *"Men would be lovers of pleasure more than lovers of God. (They would be)...covetous,...disobedient to parents, unthankful, unholy, without natural affection, trucebreakers,...heady, highminded"* (II Timothy 3:1-4).

In the Last Days, we won't be able to trust the integrity of man. Good will look evil and evil will look good to the world.

Do we not lack integrity today?!

Reich goes on to say that family, friendship and community should be closer to the core of our lives than career, wealth and status, but unfortunately that doesn't seem to be true in our lifestyles.

Americans are working longer, and more frantically than ever before. They have no time or energy left over for the things that really matter. He says that people in the 1950s wondered what we would do with all the free time new technology would allow us to have in this century.

Man, did they miss that like a barn door?!

The average American works 350 more hours a year than the average European, which is even more than the notoriously, industrious Japanese.

Only 8% of Americans said that they would prefer to work less hours for less pay, compared to 38% of Germans, 30% of Japanese and 30% of people in the United Kingdom.

People in the United States don't even want to slow down!

It's easy to see why our family life is eroding in this country. It's not rocket science.

The problem has become how to balance making a living with making a life.

The new economy offers us so many things that it's easy to feel like we have to have it all. We've never had more opportunities to work for more things.

On the flip side, just to survive, companies are forced continually to cut costs, add value, and develop better, faster, cheaper products and services of every description.

In other words, it's a frantic pace both for the consumer and the producer.

Do you see why we need to tap into God's economy and not just take what the world has to offer?

If we don't blend these two together, the world's economy will chew us up and spit us out.

Reich says America was founded by people who left places and abandoned old ways in search of a better deal. Now, every year 17% of Americans change their residences. By second grade almost 40% of all children have attended more than one school. Twenty percent of all workers change jobs each year. Many people are changing spouses.

Kids and families don't fit in easily with these new trends.

In the 1950s only 15% of the women in America with children under six were in full-time paid work. Today it's 69%. We can expect the percentage to continue to rise.

The percentage of married people with children at home in 1972 was 45%. In 1998 it was 26%.

In the 1950s 5.3% of births involved unmarried women. By the 1990s more than 32% of all births took place outside of wedlock.

The percentage of unmarried people without children during that same period of time increased from 16% up to 32%. In short, the typical household has shifted from married with children to unmarried without children.

Today about 70% of young women are heading to college compared to only 64% of male high school graduates. Among highly educated women, nearly half now earn more than their husbands.

High-powered jobs and an emerging economy demand total commitment. We have to work late with customers and clients, be available at all hours, develop our contacts and stay abreast of new developments. Most working women continue to be the major caretakers in the family, and it is almost impossible to be both the major breadwinner and the major caretaker in a home.

The new economy has us busy. We're running and we're running fast.

NO WORK WORRIES

The great news is that God hasn't left us alone. Just because the world runs at break-neck speed, we don't need to become workaholics. We need to work the right amount of time to get things done.

The Bible says, *"Six days you work, one day you rest"* (Exodus 23:12). There's nothing in the Bible about a forty-hour work week. We ought to be able to come home at a decent hour and not waste all our quality family time. That's why we have to be in control of our time. The devil will use people to steal it, so we have to learn how to be better time managers.

"How?" you ask.

Look at what God says. He's going to help us.

> *Moreover, when God gives any man wealth and possessions, and enables him to enjoy them, to accept his lot and be happy in his work—this is a gift of God. He seldom reflects on the days of his life, because God keeps him occupied with gladness of heart.*
>
> *Ecclesiastes 5:19-20 NIV*

You ought to be able to go to your job every day, be happy to go there, accept your lot, and enjoy your wealth and possessions. Enjoying life is a gift of God.

> *Unless the LORD builds the house, they labour in vain that build it....*
>
> *Psalm 127:1*

We don't want to work hard just for the sake of working hard. We want to be diligent, but we want to work where we're productive and still have time for our families, our God and our friends.

> *And the cares of this world, and the deceitfulness of riches, and the lusts of other things entering in, choke the word, and it becometh unfruitful.*
>
> *Mark 4:19*

God wants us to have stuff, but He doesn't want our stuff choking out our lives with Him and our families.

> *Thou wilt keep him in perfect peace, whose mind is stayed on thee: because he trusteth in thee.*
>
> *Isaiah 26:3*

> *Casting all your care upon him; for he careth for you.*
>
> *I Peter 5:7*

> *Be careful for nothing; but in every thing by prayer and supplication with thanksgiving let your requests be made known unto God. And the peace of God, which passeth all understanding, shall keep your hearts and minds through Christ Jesus.*
>
> *Philippians 4:6-7*

We can work hard and still have the peace of God all over us. It is possible!

> *But when ye pray, use not vain repetitions, as the heathen do: for they think that they shall be heard for their much speaking. Be not ye therefore like unto them: for your Father knoweth what things ye have need of, before ye ask him.*
>
> *Matthew 6:7-8*

Therefore take no thought, saying, What shall we eat? or, What shall we drink? or, Wherewithal shall we be clothed? (For after all these things do the Gentiles seek:) for your heavenly Father knoweth that ye have need of all these things. But seek ye first the kingdom of God, and his righteousness; and all these things shall be added unto you.

Matthew 6:31-33

I will instruct you and teach you in the way you should go; I will counsel you and watch over you.

Psalm 32:8 NIV

God will help you get the best job. He'll help you get the right knowledge. He'll help you go where you need to go.

The LORD does not let the righteous go hungry but he thwarts the craving of the wicked.

Proverbs 10:3 NIV

He's not going to let us starve or go under. I don't care if they close the company down and move overseas. When one job closes, He'll open up another. He's the God who opens doors no man can shut and shuts doors no man can open. The heart of the king is in the hand of the Lord and He can turn it wherever He wills.

What the wicked dreads will overtake him; what the righteous desire will be granted.

Proverbs 10:24 NIV

He that trusteth in his riches shall fall: but the righteous shall flourish as a branch.

Proverbs 11:28

If the righteous are rewarded here on earth, how much more true that the wicked and the sinner will get what they deserve!

Proverbs 11:31 NLT

Misfortune pursues the sinner, but prosperity is the reward of the righteous.

Proverbs 13:21 NIV

The righteous eat to their hearts' content, but the stomach of the wicked goes hungry.

Proverbs 13:25 NIV

In the house of the righteous is much treasure: but in the revenues of the wicked is trouble.

Proverbs 15:6

We have a promise in God's Word that says our houses will be full of much treasure. I don't know about you, but that makes me feel a lot better. We can trust God and not worry about the future.

But that doesn't mean we can just sit around and wait for money to fall on us out of Heaven.

THREE KINDS OF EDUCATION

Along with believing God, we need to take some natural steps to better ourselves in the job market. We should always be looking for ways to improve our education and to make ourselves more valuable.

There are three types of education that we can have which will help us to better ourselves financially. The first type of education is what everyone thinks about the most—namely **academic or scholastic education**. To do what God has called us to do, we're going to have to have—at the very least—a basic education. I know there are stories of people who had only a middle-school- or elementary-school-level education who went out and became millionaires, but those stories are few and far between and they're usually about people who made their money decades ago. It's just common sense that we need to have some basic knowledge to be successful in life.

The second type of education we can receive is **professional education**. If we are lacking in certain skills, we can better our positions with some vocational training or higher education. We can go to college, get a degree or go to a vocational school and learn a new trade or improve the skills we have. If we want to become more valuable and get paid more money, we need to become experts at what we do. The world is full of people who are jacks-of-all-trades, but masters of none. At the end of the day, those people don't bring home as much as the experts.

Finally, besides academic education and professional training, there's **financial education**. I'll be honest, that's really where we miss it most of the time.

You see, knowledge in and of itself won't get us a job or a paycheck, but once we find a place to work, we will get paid for what we know. And we need to know more tomorrow than we know today if we want to make more tomorrow than we do today.

But if we do make more money than the average person, if we don't have any financial "smarts" about us, we're going to blow everything we make.

If we don't know how to make a spending plan and stick to it—if we don't know how to prepare for a rainy day—if we don't know how to make our money make money—we'll just keep plodding along with the rest of the Joneses, barely getting by. Along with academic and professional knowledge, we have to get some financial know-how about us to survive in this economy. Those who have more education in all three realms make more money than those who don't.

Robert Reich says that people who can only do routine work will see their wages pushed down by technological advances and workers from around the world who can do the same work cheaper and faster. In other words, the disparity in earnings between average workers and professionals is going to get larger and larger.

YEARLY EARNINGS BY EDUCATION LEVEL

According to the Federal Government, education has a tremendous bearing on wages in this country. For people ages 18 and over who were employed full-time, the average yearly earnings by education level break down this way:

Less than high school	$20,388
High school diploma	$27,348
Some college	$31,368
Vocational training	$29,892
Associate's degree	$34,092
Bachelor's degree	$44,004
Master's degree	$55,620
Professional	$86,688
Doctorate	$72,564

Notice that the person with a Bachelor's degree earns over double what the average person with less than a high school education earns. Over a lifetime, that really starts to add up. If we need more education, there's not a better time than today to start getting one.

GOAL SETTING IS BIBLICAL

Now here's what we need to do. We need to set some goals in order to get where God wants us to go. Goal setting is Biblical.

The plans of the diligent lead to profit as surely as haste leads to poverty.
Proverbs 21:5 NIV

Where do we want to be five years from now?

Businesses have five-year plans. We ought to have five-year plans.

Do we want to be living in the house we're living in five years from now? Do we want to be driving the car we're driving five years from now?

If we don't, we'd better come up with a plan to do something different.

Will Rogers said it this way: ***"If you don't know where you want to go, then it doesn't matter where you end up."***

A study of Harvard graduates with MBA degrees revealed that 3% of them accomplished more in a single year than all the other 97% combined. The only differentiating characteristic was that the graduates who made up the 3% had left Harvard with written goals. John Maxwell says it like this, "Success is in the daily agenda."

Ants—they aren't strong, but they store up food for the winter.
Proverbs 30:25 NLT

If you fail to plan, you plan to fail.

VALUES VS. GOALS

In the book *Smart Couples Finish Rich* (New York, NY: Broadway Books, 2001), David Bach wrote a chapter on goal setting based on what's important to us personally. When people fail to reach their goals, many times it's because they didn't have those goals firmly rooted in their core values. They said they wanted something, but deep down inside, it wasn't really that important to them.

Values are beliefs which come from our hearts (our spirits). They are concrete and they last forever.

In planning, it's important to distinguish values from goals. Values are not the same as goals. Values are something that is vitally important to our belief system. Goals are simply a plan to help us fulfill our values in life.

As we begin to think about our core values, we'll find that the process of setting specific financial goals becomes a lot clearer. Instead of working and scraping to buy all those things we really don't want or need, all of a sudden, we find a true purpose and a meaning for achieving financial success. We have a righteous cause to work for, not just an empty pipe-dream.

One core value could be security. Freedom, happiness, peace, fun, excitement, marriage, family, friends, spiritual growth, creativity, confidence and love are all values. Your core values may not be the same as mine.

Bach asks us to go through and pick our top five values before setting our financial goals. There's a sample list of values in the book, but all we have to do is pick our top five. If we're married, we should also have our spouses pick their top five values. Once we have our top five values figured out, then we can go on to the goal-setting stage.

For example, my most important value might be security. In other words, after I retire, I want to be able to live with the same standard of living that I'm living at now. To do that, I'm going to have to retire with a million dollars in the bank, so I can live off the monthly interest that I'll make off of that. If my top value is security, I don't want to have to dip into the principal. I just want to live off the interest. So that means I need to figure out some way of getting a million dollars in the bank.

Is that impossible?

No, it's not. *(See Section Four for information on the wonders of compound interest.)*

If I determine that another one of my values is freedom, freedom to me might be to set a financial goal to pay off my mortgage, so I won't be worrying about having a place to live. I might want to have my house paid for more than anything else. Well, that's got a dollar figure attached to it and I can set a goal and begin to take steps to reach that amount.

Maybe you want to be happy, and to you being happy is being debt free. That's got a dollar figure attached to it.

Maybe you want to have fun the rest of your life. To you fun is traveling. Traveling costs money.

How often do you want to travel? Where do you want to go?

There's a dollar figure attached to that.

Maybe family's the most important thing to you. You want to spend more time with your kids. To do that you have to make more money in the time that you're working so you aren't having to work a lot of overtime to cover your obligations. Maybe you need to go back to school to improve your skills or finish your degree. Maybe you need more training.

How can you make more money and what steps do you need to take to make that work?

So we pick a value. Then we put a dollar figure to it. Once we have a dollar figure, we're ready to lay out a plan.

We need to prepare for the future. That's one of key the principles of financial security. A little saving and planning for the future will put us way ahead in life.

Once we've learned how to increase, we need to learn another key principle of financial security. That is how to make our money make money. People don't make money. Money makes money, and that's what we're going to look at in the next section.

$ection 4

the power to get wealth

Sowing And Reaping

the power
to get wealth

SOWING AND REAPING

WHAT WE NEED:

To thrive financially—not just to survive

WHY WE NEED IT:

A good man leaves an inheritance for his family.

HOW CAN WE DO IT?

We must practice the law of seed time and harvest.

Money makes money. In this section, we will study the principles of increase through tithing, giving, sowing and reaping, lending and investing. The blessings of God follow obedience to the laws of God. His will for His people is for them to obey His Word.

> *Always remember that it is the Lord your God who gives you power to become rich, and he does it to fulfill his promise to your ancestors.*
> *Deuteronomy 8:18 TLB*

THERE WILL ALWAYS BE AN ECONOMY

While the earth remaineth, seedtime and harvest, and cold and heat, and summer and winter, and day and night shall not cease.

Genesis 8:22

Faith is fluid. Some days we have it. Some days we don't. One day we may have great faith. One day we may have no faith. That's because faith is fluid. It changes. That's why we have the Word of God. The more we get into the Word of God, the more we can build our faith. *Faith comes by hearing and hearing by the Word of God* (Romans 10:17).

Money is like faith. It is fluid. Just because we don't have it, that doesn't mean we can't get it. And just because we have a lot of money today, that doesn't mean we're going to hold on to it tomorrow. Money flows. It's either flowing toward us or it's moving away from us.

Now here's what we need to understand about the flow of money. As long as people exist, there will always be an economy. Money will be flowing to and from people as long as the world stands.

There will be wars and rumors of wars. There will be pestilence, earthquakes and famine. The Last Days will be perilous times. But where sin is abounding, the Bible says that grace will *much more abound.*

That means that somebody is going to be thriving in the Last Days because that's when the harvest is taking place. When the former and the latter rain are coming together and there's a tremendous outpouring of God's power, this wonderful Gospel will be preached to the four corners of the earth.

That's why I think the greatest economy in the Last Days is going to be connected to the Gospel. Jesus said, *"This Gospel will be preached."* No ifs, ands, or buts—it's going to be done, and it's going to take money to do it. It takes money to preach the Gospel. It takes money to build buildings, to fly planes, to send preachers, to print material, to make CDs, tapes and books. It takes money to help the poor.

That means God is going to have people somewhere is this world who are great givers. *But you can't be a great giver, if you're not a great getter.*

That's some powerful revelation for the people of God who are alive in the Last Days!

That knowledge should help every man and woman of God—every Christian family, every believing businessman—to increase what they're doing.

God is trying to wake up the Body of Christ to get us to believe for more—more than just to have our needs met. He also wants us to be able to **give abundantly** beyond that. To always be ready and able to give to every good work.

> *"[When I return] the world will be [as indifferent to the things of God] as the people were in Noah's day. They ate and drank and married—everything just as usual right up to the day when Noah went into the Ark and the flood came and destroyed them all. And it will be as it was in the days of Lot: people went about their daily business—eating and drinking, buying and selling, farming and building—until the morning Lot left Sodom. Then fire and brimstone rained down from heaven and destroyed them all. Yes, it will be 'business as usual' right up to the hour of my return."*
>
> *Luke 17:26-30 TLB*

GOD EXPECTS INCREASE

God didn't just save us. He saved us so we could save others. He didn't just bless us. He blessed us so we could bless others. God expects increase in every area of our lives.

> *And other fell on good ground, and did yield fruit that sprang up and increased; and brought forth, some thirty, and some sixty, and some an hundred.*
>
> *Mark 4:8*

> *And Jesus answered and said, Verily I say unto you, There is no man that hath left house, or brethren, or sisters, or father, or mother, or wife, or children, or lands, for my sake, and the gospel's, But he shall receive an hundredfold now in this time, houses, and brethren, and sisters, and mothers, and children, and lands, with persecutions; and in the world to come eternal life.*
>
> *Mark 10:29-30*

> *I am the vine, ye are the branches: He that abideth in me, and I in him, the same bringeth forth much fruit: for without me ye can do nothing. If a man abide not in me, he is cast forth as a branch, and is withered; and men gather them, and cast them into the fire, and they are burned.*
>
> *John 15:5-6*

> *Herein is my Father glorified, that ye bear much fruit; so shall ye be my disciples.*
>
> *John 15:8*

Verily, verily, I say unto you, Except a corn of wheat fall into the ground and die, it abideth alone: but if it die, it bringeth forth much fruit.

John 12:24

That ye might walk worthy of the Lord unto all pleasing, being fruitful in every good work, and increasing in the knowledge of God...

Colossians 1:10

Now unto him that is able to do exceeding abundantly above all that we ask or think, according to the power that worketh in us...

Ephesians 3:20

Honour the LORD with thy substance, and with the firstfruits of all thine increase: So shall thy barns be filled with plenty, and thy presses shall burst out with new wine.

Proverbs 3:9-10

So then neither is he that planteth any thing, neither he that watereth; but God that giveth the increase.

I Corinthians 3:7

Now he who supplies seed to the sower and bread for food will also supply and increase your store of seed and will enlarge the harvest of your righteousness. You will be made rich in every way so that you can be generous on every occasion, and through us your generosity will result in thanksgiving to God.

II Corinthians 9:10-11 NIV

God expects us to be good stewards over what He has given us and that means we must increase. A faithful servant is not someone who hangs on to what he has for dear life. A faithful servant is someone who multiplies what he's a steward over.

God expects increase.

PERSONAL WEALTH IN AMERICA

I covered the statistics earlier, but I want to point out here that there's a great disparity between what God says in His Word about financial increase and what most Christians believe. In the very first section of the book, I said that the majority of people ages 65 and over will retire below poverty level, yet 87% of those same people in America claim to be evangelical Christians.

We believe in God, but we're retiring broke.

What kind of a God is that?

What are we expecting out of Him?

He's expecting something out of us.

He's expecting us to increase and multiply what He's given us. So we ought to be expecting God to bless us. The promises are there in His Word.

So why aren't we tapping into them?

To be sure, there are some people who have a different mindset in this country. They know how to tap into prosperity. Here are some conflicting statistics.

The Wealthy—There has never been more personal wealth in America than there is today (over $22 trillion).

Average America—Without Social Security benefits, almost half of all Americans over age 65 would live in poverty.

The Wealthy—Half of America's wealth is owned by 3.5% of our households.

Average America—Only a minority of Americans have even the most conventional types of financial assets.

WHERE ARE OUR ASSETS?

- 15% of American households have a money-market deposit account.

- 22% have one or more certificates of deposit (CDs).

- 4.2% have money invested in a money-market fund.

- 3.4% own any type of corporate or municipal bonds.

- 25% of households own shares of individual stocks and/or mutual funds.

- 8.4% own rental property.

- 18.1% of American households own U.S. Savings Bonds

- 23% of have IRA or KEOGH accounts.

- 65% of households have some amount of equity in their own homes.

- 85% of all the households in this country own one or more vehicles.

- The median household in America has a net worth of less than $15,000, excluding home equity.

- Factoring out equity (in motor vehicles, furniture and the like), most households have no financial assets—that's zero—such as stocks, bonds, savings accounts!

How long could the average American household survive without a regular paycheck from an employer? How long can they last without going belly up?

The answer is not long—not long at all.

WHO IS RICH?

Of the $22 trillion dollars in America, half of that ($11 trillion) is concentrated in 3.5% of the households in this country. Somebody's learning how to manage wealth. I don't know if those people know God or not, but they've learned how to move and grow money.

In fact these people are not just people who have inherited their money. The government says that over 80% of all millionaires are brand new millionaires. They didn't inherit their money. They didn't get it with "get-rich-quick" schemes. They made new money. It happens all the time.

The government breaks it down for us.

Based upon the year 2000 dollar valuations, upon retirement at age 65:

CLASSIFICATION	HOUSEHOLD INCOME
Poor	$25,000 or less per year
Middle-Class	$25,000 to $100,000 per year
Affluent	$100,000 to $1 million per year
Rich	$1 million or more per year
Ultra-Rich	$1 million or more per month

What category do you fall in?

As believers we need to remember what God says in His Word. It says we're blessed. Wealth and riches will be in our houses. We just need to get some knowledge and steward what God has given us so we can receive our blessings and use them to bless others.

> *Praise ye the LORD. Blessed is the man that feareth the LORD, that delighteth greatly in his commandments. His seed shall be mighty upon earth: the generation of the upright shall be blessed. Wealth and riches shall be in his*

house: and his righteousness endureth for ever.

Psalm 112:1-3

The blessing of the LORD, it maketh rich, and he addeth no sorrow with it.

Proverbs 10:22

Charge them that are rich in this world, that they be not highminded, nor trust in uncertain riches, but in the living God, who giveth us richly all things to enjoy; That they do good, that they be rich in good works, ready to distribute, willing to communicate; Laying up in store for themselves a good foundation against the time to come, that they may lay hold on eternal life.

I Timothy 6:17-19

THE AVERAGE MILLIONAIRE

If we've never had money, we might have some wrong ideas about rich people—who they are, what they do, what they don't do. That's why I love the book *The Millionaire Mind* (Kansas City, MO: Andrews McMeel Publishing, 2000) written by Thomas J. Stanley and the book *The Millionaire Next Door: The Surprising Secrets Of America's Wealth* (Atlanta, GA: Longstreet Press, 1996) co-written by Stanley and William D. Danko.

How do millionaires live? What do they buy? What don't they buy?

Most millionaires think differently than the rest of the us.

According to Stanley and Danko, the typical American millionaire is a man who has a net worth of about $4.3 million with a median annual income of just over $430,000. He is in his fifties, has been married to the same woman for 25 years or more and has three kids.

Although those statistics aren't surprising, there are some unexpected discoveries that Stanley and Danko made about the millionaires of this country.

For example, the typical American millionaire has never spent more that $41,000 for a car. The purchase price of the average millionaire's home twelve years ago (when they bought it) was just over $400,000. The current average value of that home today is $1.4 million, yet they have a small mortgage if any. One in every four millionaires have never spent more than $24 for a haircut.

As for millionaires' occupations, 32% are business owners, 16% are senior corporate executives, 10% are attorneys, 9% are physicians and the remaining 33% are divided among retirees, corporate middle managers, accountants, salesmen, engineers, architects, teachers and housewives. Ninety percent of millionaires are college graduates. Nearly 50% of male millionaire's wives do not work outside of the home.

There are also three characteristics that almost all millionaires have in common.

1. **They live below their means.**

2. **They invest at least 10% of all they earn and hold it for the future (retirement).**

3. **They pay top dollar for good professional advice about taxes and investments.**

American millionaires have made themselves financially independent, and most live comfortable—but *not extravagant*—lifestyles.

I believe all of God's children can become millionaires. It doesn't take a lot of money to do it if we get our money working for us early. But if we have ten credit cards charged to the max and we're paying 18.9% interest, we're not going to be millionaires. We're not going to be anything but broke!

Our money will be flowing in the wrong direction. We'll be paying somebody else to use their money, so somebody can pay them to use our money. We've got to reverse that flow!

WEALTH LEAKAGE

If we want to become wealthy, it's important to pay as much attention to the money that leaks from our wallets as we do to the rate of return on our investments.

In other words, if we earn $40,000 and invest 10% of that ($4,000), trimming our expenses by only 1% of our income would have the same effect as getting a 10% return on our $4,000 investment.

Did you catch all that?

Trimming 1% gets us the equivalent of 10% on our investment. Let's do the math.

Our annual earnings	$40,000
Reducing our expenses by 1% of our earnings gets us	$400
Investing $4,000 with a 10% annual rate of return gets us	$4,400*

Our $4,000 original investment plus a 10% return of $400

There's nowhere I know of that we can get a *guaranteed* rate of return on stocks or bonds of 10%, but if we cut our expenses by only 1%, it automatically has that effect.

If we don't find and plug the leaks in our spending, our only other alternatives will be to sell some stuff to get more money, to work longer hours (some of us work 60 hours a week as it is), or to take more risks with our investments in hopes that we'll get higher returns. That could put us in a precarious financial position.

By far the easiest and least painful way to make more money available for investments is to stop the leaks in our expense column. These three areas are the places where people are most likely to overspend.

1. **Interest On Debts**—We've already covered how to pay our debts down. We need to get that interest money coming to us, not going away from us.

2. **Taxes**—We might be able to invest $500 in an IRA at the end of the year and drop our tax bracket from 35% to 28% and save $2,000 just by investing $500.

3. **Insurance Costs**—This is one area where if we don't do the research, it will cost us big. *(Go back and review the section on insurance if you haven't already plugged this leak.)*

NEGLECTED GIVING

With that said, I believe there is one area where we shouldn't cut back. That's in our giving. That's a sure way to end up in poverty.

Do you remember how many times the word give was in the Bible?

It's there 2,162 times. It's important to be a giver. Giving keeps the pipes from Heaven unclogged. Giving keeps us from being stingy and choking off the flow of blessing.

Take a look at the following facts about giving in America:

*   More money is spent on chewing gum, or dog food in the United States than is given to foreign missions.

*   Americans on average—believers and non-believers—give less than 1.7% of their adjusted gross income as charitable contributions.

- The average Christian gives approximately 2% (far below the tithe).

How are we going to go from just surviving to thriving?

The same way the children of Israel did when they crossed the Jordan River.

How did they go from the land of just enough to the land of more than enough?

They planted seed. They left the land of manna and the great miracle of God feeding them without them having to do anything to go into the land of seedtime and harvest where they could eat their own roasted grain (Joshua 5:10-12). They could plant as many crops as they wanted. They got to determine how much increase they wanted. If they sowed bountifully, they reaped bountifully. If they sowed sparingly, they reaped sparingly (II Corinthians 9:6).

With what measure we meet, it will be measured to us again (Luke 6:38). The seed we plant determines our harvest.

TITHING: THE DOORWAY TO INCREASE

Now we're going to be stepping things up a notch. We're going to be talking about how we receive the power to get wealth by honoring God and His Word.

Before you close the book right here, let me say that I know tithing is a controversial subject. You bring it up and nobody wants to talk about it. But I'm telling you that I'm going to approach tithing from some different viewpoints. Maybe I'll cover some verses in the Bible or some principles you've never seen or heard. Or maybe you think you know all there is to know about this subject—but I'm telling you, if you want to have financial increase in your life, *do not skip over this section of the book!*

> *Bring this tithe to eat before the Lord your God at the place he shall choose as his sanctuary; this applies to your tithes of grain, new wine, olive oil, and the firstborn of your flocks and herds. The purpose of tithing is to teach you always to put God first in your lives.*
>
> *Deuteronomy 14:23 TLB*

There it is in black and white. *The purpose of tithing is to teach us always to put God first in our lives.*

There is no other purpose for tithing. God doesn't need our money. God already owns everything on this planet. Tithing is a constant reminder that all our increase—everything we have—comes from Him.

SIX EXCUSES PEOPLE GIVE FOR NOT TITHING

1. We can't afford to tithe.

2. Let someone else support the church.

3. Pastors are greedy and should get real jobs.

4. I can pay my tithes anywhere I want.

5. I will tithe if I have any money left over after I pay all my other bills.

6. Tithing was under the Law and it isn't valid in the New Testament.

UNDER THE LAW?

> *And blessed be the most high God, which hath delivered thine enemies into thy hand. And he (Abram) gave him tithes of all.*
>
> *Genesis 14:20 (author's note)*

> *Consider then how great this Melchizedek was. Even Abraham, the great patriarch of Israel, recognized how great Melchizedek was by giving him a tenth of what he had taken in battle.*
>
> *Hebrews 7:4 NLT*

In Genesis we see the first mention of tithing in the Bible. Abram—before he was called Abraham—the father of our faith, gave tithes to the high priest Melchizedek.

Abram had been minding his own business, and all of a sudden some kings invaded the land where Lot, his nephew, lived. They had stolen Lot's family and all of his goods and carried them off. Abram heard about it, and he took his servants and went after the kings. Abram not only rescued Lot and his family and got their stuff back, but he also got a lot of spoil from the kings themselves.

On Abram's way back home Melchizedek the high priest met him on the road. Melchizedek blessed Abram, and Abram paid him tithes on everything he had taken in battle. ***Four hundred and thirty years before the Law of Moses, Abram paid his tithe.***

Jacob tithed. He first promised to do it when he wrestled with the angel (Genesis 28:22). He didn't have the Law, yet he promised to give a tenth of everything he received to God.

Tithing was before the Law, during the Law and after the Law.

"How terrible it will be for you teachers of religious law and you Pharisees. Hypocrites! For you are careful to tithe even the tiniest part of your income, but you ignore the important things of the law—justice, mercy, and faith. You should tithe, Yes, but you should not leave undone the more important things."

Matthew 23:23 NLT

Notice Jesus didn't tell these Pharisees not to tithe. He said, "Yes, tithing is important—but you also shouldn't be neglecting the important things of the law like justice, forgiveness and faith." He said they needed to include those things **with their tithes.** He didn't say they shouldn't tithe.

And here men that die receive tithes; but there he receiveth them, of whom it is witnessed that he liveth.

Hebrews 7:8

Tithing affects both the earth's economy and God's economy. Men get our money, but Jesus, our great High Priest, gets our faith when we tithe.

GIVE GOD THE FIRST AND THE BEST

And all the tithe of the land, whether of the seed of the land, or of the fruit of the tree, is the LORD'S: it is holy unto the LORD.

Leviticus 27:30

Thou shalt truly tithe all the increase of thy seed, that the field bringeth forth year by year.

Deuteronomy 14:22

That thou shalt take of the first of all the fruit of the earth, which thou shalt bring of thy land that the LORD thy God giveth thee, and shalt put it in a basket, and shalt go unto the place which the LORD thy God shall choose to place his name there.

Deuteronomy 26:2

All the best of the oil, and all the best of the wine, and of the wheat, the firstfruits of them which they shall offer unto the LORD, them have I given thee.

Numbers 18:12

And as soon as the commandment came abroad, the children of Israel brought in abundance the firstfruits of corn, wine, and oil, and honey, and of all the increase of the field; and the tithe of all things brought they in abundantly.

II Chronicles 31:5

"Is it a time for you yourselves to be living in your paneled houses, while this house remains a ruin?" Now this is what the LORD Almighty says: "Give careful thought to your ways. You have planted much, but have harvested little.

You eat, but never have enough. You drink, but never have your fill. You put on clothes, but are not warm. You earn wages, only to put them in a purse with holes in it." This is what the LORD Almighty says: "Give careful thought to your ways. Go up into the mountains and bring down timber and build the house, so that I may take pleasure in it and be honored," says the LORD. "You expected much, but see, it turned out to be little. What you brought home, I blew away. Why?" declares the LORD Almighty. "Because of my house, which remains a ruin, while each of you is busy with his own house.

Haggai 1:4-9 NIV

A son honoureth his father, and a servant his master: if then I be a father, where is mine honour? and if I be a master, where is my fear? saith the LORD of hosts unto you...

Malachi 1:6

But my name is honored by people of other nations from morning till night. All around the world they offer sweet incense and pure offerings in honor of my name. For my name is great among the nations," says the LORD Almighty. "But you dishonor my name with your actions. By bringing contemptible food, you are saying it's all right to defile the Lord's table. You say, 'It's too hard to serve the LORD,' and you turn up your noses at his commands," says the LORD Almighty. "Think of it! Animals that are stolen and mutilated, crippled and sick—presented as offerings! Should I accept from you such offerings as these?" asks the LORD. "Cursed is the cheat who promises to give a fine ram from his flock but then sacrifices a defective one to the Lord. For I am a great king," says the LORD Almighty, "and my name is feared among the nations!"

Malachi 1:11-14 NLT

Will a man rob God? Yet ye have robbed me. But ye say, Wherein have we robbed thee? In tithes and offerings. Ye are cursed with a curse: for ye have robbed me, even this whole nation. Bring ye all the tithes into the storehouse, that there may be meat in mine house, and prove me now herewith, saith the LORD of hosts, if I will not open you the windows of heaven, and pour you out a blessing, that there shall not be room enough to receive it. And I will rebuke the devourer for your sakes, and he shall not destroy the fruits of your ground; neither shall your vine cast her fruit before the time in the field, saith the LORD of hosts. And all nations shall call you blessed: for ye shall be a delightsome land, saith the LORD of hosts.

Malachi 3:8-12

THE BENEFITS OF TITHING

If you're not a tither, and you're sitting out there reading this chapter, all I can tell you is this: ***Study these scriptures and just pray about tithing for thirty days.***

I'm not your pastor. You don't have to do what I tell you. You don't have to give anything to me. Your tithe should go to your local church. I'm not getting one thing out of this, but I'm trying to teach you as a brother in the Lord how to bring financial blessings on your household. That's all I'm doing.

You just take a month and pray about it. You don't have to do anything today, tomorrow or even next week. Don't do anything out of condemnation. If you're condemned, that's the devil. Believers should do things out of conviction, not out of condemnation.

God loves you. God loves everybody in the world—saints, sinners, tithers *and non-tithers.*

Because He loves you, here's what I believe. You are God's sheep. He is your Shepherd. You will hear His voice. The voice of a stranger you will not follow (John 10:4-5). God will talk to you when you sleep at night, when you get up in the morning and when you walk in the way (Proverbs 6:22).

God is good enough that once you've got the seed of the Word on the inside of you about this, I believe God will help you. God wants to bring you abundant blessing. There is only one place in the Bible where God said, "Test Me on this. See if I won't bless you" (Malachi 3:10).

That's because we can't make it on our own. We've got to get God involved in our finances. Just look at all the benefits we'll get by being tithers.

- We remove ourselves from the list of those who rob God (Malachi 3:8).

- We free ourselves from the curse (Malachi 3:9).

- The windows of Heaven will be opened for us (Malachi 3:10).

- God will pour out a blessing on us (Malachi 3:10).

- We won't have room to contain all the blessings He gives us (Malachi 3:10).

- God will rebuke the devourer for our sakes (Malachi 3:11).

- The fruit of our ground will not be destroyed (Malachi 3:11).

- All people will call us blessed (Malachi 3:12).

- We will be a delightful household (Malachi 3:12).

- Our names will be written in God's Book of Remembrance (Malachi 3:16).

- We will be fruitful and have increase (Leviticus 26:3-5).

- The Lord will give us the power to get wealth (Deuteronomy 8:18).

- We will eat the good of the land (Isaiah 1:19).

- Our houses, our cupboards and our closets will be filled with plenty (Proverbs 3:10).

THINGS WHICH CAN HURT YOUR TITHE

- Mourning over the giving of your tithe (Malachi 3:14)

- Doubting the value of God's system (Malachi 3:14)

- Growing weary and tithing sporadically (Galatians 6:9)

- Speaking wrong words over your giving (Malachi 2:13, 17)

- Poor stewardship of your money (Luke 16:10-13)

THE TITHE IS HOLY

In the Book of Joshua, we have a picture of the tithe as something that is sanctified and set apart for God. The Lord reinstituted—or reconfirmed—three very important sacraments for His people in this story.

In Joshua chapter 5, Joshua had just crossed over the Jordan River and the children of Israel were about to storm the city of Jericho and take the Promised Land. But first, Joshua circumcised all the males who had not been circumcised in the wilderness as a sign that they were part of the covenant with God. Circumcision is the first sacrament that God reconfirmed before the children went in to the Land of Canaan.

The counterpart to circumcision today would be water baptism. We go down into the water to show that our old man has died with Christ and that our new man has been raised with Him. Water baptism demonstrates that our old man is dead and we are now in covenant with God.

Now look at the second thing God had Joshua do.

> *While the Israelites were camped at Gilgal on the plains of Jericho, they celebrated Passover on the evening of the fourteenth day of the first month—the month that marked their exodus from Egypt. The very next day they began to*

eat unleavened bread and roasted grain harvested from the land. No manna appeared that day, and it was never seen again. So from that time on the Israelites ate from the crops of Canaan.

Joshua 5:10-12 NLT

God reconfirmed Passover.

Now what's the New Testament parallel to that?

It's the Lord's Supper.

Why do we take the Lord's Supper?

To remind us. *"Do this in remembrance of Me...,"* Jesus said. When we partake of the Lord's Supper, we remember that the blood of Jesus was shed for us. When we remember that Jesus died on the cross for us, we also remember that we have been redeemed from the curse of the Law, for cursed is everyone who hangs on a tree (Galatians 3:13). When we take communion, we're reminding ourselves that we are free from the curse and have all the benefits—the blessings—of the covenant because of Christ.

As soon as the children of Israel celebrated Passover, notice that the manna disappeared. God was getting ready to reinstitute the third sacrament—the one which was going to take them into the land of more than enough.

> *On the seventh day, they got up at daybreak and marched around the city seven times in the same manner, except that on that day they circled the city seven times. The seventh time around, when the priests sounded the trumpet blast, Joshua commanded the people, "Shout! For the LORD has given you the city! The city and all that is in it are to be devoted to the LORD. Only Rahab the prostitute and all who are with her in her house shall be spared, because she hid the spies we sent. But keep away from the devoted things, so that you will not bring about your own destruction by taking any of them. Otherwise you will make the camp of Israel liable to destruction and bring trouble on it."*
>
> *Joshua 6:15-18 NIV*

God told Joshua that the city of Jericho was **devoted,** or dedicated, to Him for a sacrifice. Jericho was the first city the children of Israel were going to take in Canaan. With its destruction, the third sacrament God reconfirmed was the sacrament of tithing. **Jericho represented the tithe of all of the cities of the Promised Land.** Jericho and everything in it belonged to Him.

In the King James version, the word *devoted* in the New International version is translated *accursed.* (See also Leviticus 27:21 and 28.) The word in Hebrew is *charem*—it's where we get our word *harem.* A harem was where a middle-eastern man kept his wife or wives. It was private. To go into another man's harem was punishable by death. God used that same word to describe His tithe from the Promised Land. "Don't touch this," He said. "It belongs to Me."

> *"All the silver and gold and the articles of bronze and iron are sacred to the LORD and must go into his treasury."*
>
> *Joshua 6:19 NIV*

The word *treasury* here is the same Hebrew word found in Malachi 3:10 where God says we're to bring all the tithes into His *storehouse*. **We're to bring our tithes into the local church.**

You know the rest of the story. Achan took some of the spoil from Jericho and hid it in his tent. The next time Israel went to battle—against the little town of Ai—Israel was soundly defeated.

When Joshua cried out to the Lord, the Lord answered him.

> *"...Get up! Why are you lying on your face like this? Israel has sinned and broken my covenant! They have stolen the things that I commanded to be set apart for me. And they have not only stolen them; they have also lied about it and hidden the things among their belongings. That is why the Israelites are running from their enemies in defeat. For now Israel has been set apart for destruction. I will not remain with you any longer unless you destroy the things among you that were set apart for destruction."*
>
> *Joshua 7:10-12 NLT*

God said. "You took what belonged to Me. It was Mine. It was My honor, and you took it." He said, "As long as you hold back what belongs to Me, I won't stay with you. You've put yourselves under a curse."

The next morning, Joshua assembled all the tribes and families of Judah together and one by one, as each family presented themselves to the Lord, Achan was singled out and he confessed. Joshua went and found the stolen spoil in Achan's tent.

> *Then Joshua said to Achan, "Why have you brought trouble on us? The LORD will now bring trouble on you." And all the Israelites stoned Achan and his family and burned their bodies. They piled a great heap of stones over Achan, which remains to this day....*
>
> *Joshua 7:25-26 NLT*

I know that seems like such a hard word, but God was setting a precedent. He had given a commandment about the tithe saying, "It belongs to Me," but Achan took it.

Now here's the thing we need to understand. God wasn't trying to keep stuff from His people. He wasn't trying to keep them from being blessed or from getting a reward for their work.

Look at the very next chapter:

> *Then the LORD said to Joshua, "Do not be afraid or discouraged. Take the entire army and attack Ai, for I have given to you the king of Ai, his people, his city, and his land. You will destroy them as you destroyed Jericho and its king. But this time you may keep the captured goods and the cattle for yourselves...."*
>
> *Joshua 8:1-2 NLT*

In other words, God said, "Look. I know this struck fear in everybody's heart. This has everyone worried, but don't be afraid. Don't be discouraged. I'm still with you."

After the battle was over, the Bible goes on to say:

> *So the entire population of Ai was wiped out that day—twelve thousand in all. For Joshua kept holding out his spear until everyone who had lived in Ai was completely destroyed. Only the cattle and the treasures of the city were not destroyed, for the Israelites kept these for themselves, as the LORD had commanded Joshua.*
>
> *Joshua 8:25-27 NLT*

God wanted to bless His people all along. He was just showing them that the way to get blessed is by honoring Him. We bring prosperity to our lives when we give God something first. When we put His kingdom before our own needs, He'll see to it that we walk in abundance (Matthew 6:33).

> *For I am the LORD, I change not....*
>
> *Malachi 3:6*

Tithing is a principle that transcends time. The purpose of tithing is to remind us to always fear God. With Him all things are possible, and by Him all things are held together. When we pay our tithes, we're giving God honor. In return, the windows of Heaven will be opened to us, the Lord will give us the power to get wealth and we will eat the good of the land.

JOHN D. ROCKEFELLER

Almost everybody has heard of the Rockefellers and the Rockefeller Foundation but few people know that the secret of John D. Rockefeller's wealth was his obedience in tithing.

John D. Rockefeller was born on a farm in 1839. His father was a charlatan and a womanizer. But beginning with his first job when Rockefeller earned only 60¢ a day as an errand boy, he tithed 10% of his income to the church. While working in a hay and grain company, he started an oil business on the side. By 1880, Rockefeller controlled 95% of America's oil production. *In 1905, his yearly tithe was nearly $100 million!*

Rockefeller started off with nothing. He inherited nothing. Nobody stuck a silver spoon in his mouth. All he did was obey the laws of God concerning tithing, and God opened up the windows of Heaven and poured out a blessing that he would not have room enough to contain.

When questioned about the source of his wealth, he replied, "God gave me my money. I believe the power to make money is a gift from God. It is my duty to make money and still more money and to use the money I make for the good of my fellow man." Rockefeller's net worth was estimated at $1.4 billion dollars when he died at the ripe old age of 98.

God's promises to the obedient are true.

> *If they obey and serve Him, they shall spend their days in prosperity, and their years in pleasures.*
>
> *Job 36:11*

> *Those who love me inherit wealth, for I fill their treasuries.*
>
> *Proverbs 8:21*

> *If ye be willing and obedient, ye shall eat the good of the land.*
>
> *Isaiah 1:19*

THE LAW OF SOWING AND REAPING

> *Remember this: Whoever sows sparingly will also reap sparingly, and whoever sows generously will also reap generously. Each man should give what he has decided in his heart to give, not reluctantly or under compulsion, for God loves a cheerful giver. And God is able to make all grace abound to you, so that in all things at all times, having all that you need, you will abound in every good work.*
>
> *II Corinthians 9:6-8 NIV*

> *Now he who supplies seed to the sower and bread for food will also supply and increase your store of seed and will enlarge the harvest of your righteousness.*
> *II Corinthians 9:10 NIV*

God is going to supply seed *to the sower,* not to the person who just *wants* to sow. Once we put our hands to giving, God will increase us. He's not going to steal from us. He's going to increase our seed and enlarge the harvest of our righteousness.

> Yes, God will give you much so that you can give away much, and when we take your gifts to those who need them they will break out into thanksgiving and praise to God for your help. So, two good things happen as a result of your gifts—those in need are helped, and they overflow with thanks to God.
> II Corinthians 9:11-12 TLB

> Be not deceived; God is not mocked: for whatsoever a man soweth, that shall he also reap.
> Galatians 6:7

> Give, and it shall be given unto you; good measure, pressed down, and shaken together, and running over, shall men give into your bosom. For with the same measure that ye mete withal it shall be measured to you again.
> Luke 6:38

> Cast your bread upon the waters, for after many days you will find it again.
> Ecclesiastes 11:1 NIV

> A generous man will prosper; he who refreshes others will himself be refreshed.
> Proverbs 11:25 NIV

> The sluggard's craving will be the death of him, because his hands refuse to work. All day long he craves for more, but the righteous give without sparing.
> Proverbs 21:25-26 NIV

> A generous man will himself be blessed, for he shares his food with the poor.
> Proverbs 22:9 NIV

Being a giver keeps the pipes clean.

Do we want to have wealth and not just just enough to get by?

Then we're going to have to get into the habit of giving. We're going to have to listen to God so we can sow seed, plant financial crops and bring in the harvest.

WANT TO GROW FINANCIALLY?

Everything we have today is a result of the fact that we're doing everything we know. If we ever expect to have anything other than what we currently have, we'll have to learn something we currently don't know. That means we might have to get around some other people besides the people we fellowship with right now. Whenever we see someone more successful than we are, it's because they're doing something we aren't doing.

He that walketh with wise men shall be wise: but a companion of fools shall be destroyed.

Proverbs 13:20

We have to seek out people who are responsible because we want to become more responsible. We need to find people who are great stewards because we want to be better stewards. We need to be around people who are big givers. We want to leave behind good things for our children and our children's children. We don't want to leave them debts and a bad name. We need to learn more about prosperity from people who are prosperous so we can become more prosperous.

10% of what we learn comes from what we read

20% of what we learn comes from what we hear

30% of what we learn comes from what we see

50% of what we learn comes from what we see and hear

70% of what we learn comes from what we discuss with others

80% of what we learn comes from what we personally experience

90% of what we learn comes from what we teach to others

Who do we spend our time talking with? Who do we discuss money matters with?

If it's someone who's barely getting by, we're not going to learn how to prosper. We're not going to learn anything except how to barely get by. That's not what God wants for us. He wants us to find people who can challenge us and help us move to a higher level of blessing.

Iron sharpeneth iron; so a man sharpeneth the countenance of his friend.

Proverbs 27:17

HOW TO BECOME A MILLIONAIRE
ENDURANCE BRINGS WEALTH

Dishonest money dwindles away, but he who gathers money little by little makes it grow.

Proverbs 13:11 NIV

Saving for retirement involves building wealth the slow way.

Most people say that a million dollars is the magic number when it comes to having enough money in the bank to live comfortably off of the interest after retirement and not have to dip into the principal.

So what does it take to retire with a million bucks in the bank?

That depends on our rate of return and how long our money can grow for us.

The calculations below are based on a 9%, a 10% and an 11% rate of return. (The stock market's average yearly return was right at 12% in the last century.)

If we want to be more conservative, here's what we would have to invest each year at 9% to reach a million dollars. *(To figure out how much to put back monthly, divide the annual investment amount by 12.)*

At a 9% rate of return before taxes, if we started:

At age 20, an annual investment of $1,903   gives us $1,000,709 at age 65.
At age 25, "   "   "   " $2,960   " " $1,000,132.
At age 30, "   "   "   " $4,636   " " $1,000,035.
At age 35, "   "   "   " $7,337   " " $1,000,088.
At age 40, "   "   "   " $11,807   " " $1,000,063.
At age 45, "   "   "   " $19,547   " " $1,000,027.
At age 50, "   "   "   " $34,060   " " $1,000,033.
At age 55, "   "   "   " $65,826   " " $1,000,090.
At age 60, "   "   "   "$167,100   " " $1,000,045.

Now let's add 1% to the rate of return on our investment.

At a 10% rate of return before taxes, here's where we would stand, if we started putting money back:

At age 20, an annual investment of $1,392   gives us $1,000,716 at age 65.
At age 25, "   "   "   " $2,260   " " $1,000,259.
At age 30, "   "   "   " $3,690   " " $1,000,080.
At age 35, "   "   "   " $6,080   " " $1,000,124.
At age 40, "   "   "   " $10,169   " " $1,000,091.
At age 45, "   "   "   " $17,460   " " $1,000,021.
At age 50, "   "   "   " $31,475   " " $1,000,039.
At age 55 "   "   "   " $62,750   " " $1,000,073.
At age 60, "   "   "   "$163,800   " " $1,000,015.

If we increase the rate of return on our investment to 11%, let's see what happens.

At 11% before taxes, if we started saving:

At age 20, an annual investment of $1,014   gives us $1,000,452 at age 65.

At age 25, ”   ”   ”   ” $1,719   ” ” $1,000,159.

At age 30, ”   ”   ”   ” $2,928   ” ” $1,000,174.

At age 35, ”   ”   ”   ” $5,025   ” ” $1,000,080.

At age 40, ”   ”   ”   ” $8,741   ” ” $1,000,087.

At age 45, ”   ”   ”   ” $15,577   ” ” $1,000,088.

At age 50, ”   ”   ”   ” $29,067   ” ” $1,000,061.

At age 55, ”   ”   ”   ” $59,807   ” ” $1,000,093.

At age 60, ”   ”   ”   ”$160,571   ” ” $1,000,004.

What's the key to retiring a millionaire?

It's to start early!

But even if we're already 40 or 50, it's not impossible. At age 40, we'll just have to scrape up an extra $8,741 a year to invest at 11% interest. That's only $168 a week. (That may seem like a lot, but it is possible.)

At age 50, we'll have to find $29,067 a year to invest or find a better rate of return than 11%. We may have to eat peanut butter and jelly for fifteen years, but it's not impossible. We can still do it. Even if we don't make it all the way to a million bucks, *anything* is better than nothing at all.

COMPOUND INTEREST: THE EIGHTH WONDER OF THE WORLD

Once someone asked Albert Einstein, "What is the greatest scientific discovery of the world?"

He never hesitated for one moment. He answered, "The magic of compounding interest is truly the eighth wonder of the world."

Fortunately we don't have to be scientists to put the magic of compound interest to work for us. All we have to do is follow two basic principles.

1. **Earn little by little.**

2. **Save little by little.**

If we could accumulate $10,000 in a tax-deferred account and let it grow at a 9% interest rate without any further contributions for the next 40 years, it would be worth $314,094, $650,009 at an 11% rate, or just under $1 million at 12%*.

If we could put $2,000 away into a tax-deferred account every year, at the end of 40 years we would have $675,765 at a 9% return, $1.1 million at 11%, or more than $1.5 million at 12%*.

The money would have to be invested in a tax-free or tax-deferred plan such as an IRA, a 401(k), a retirement annuity, or certain types of government bonds.

How can such small investments add up to such large amounts?

It's because money makes money.

When we get our money working for us *making* interest, instead of having credit cards charged up to the max *paying* interest, the exponential curve of compounding works *for* us and brings us wealth.

I don't know about you, but nobody ever told me when I was a kid that *anybody* could become a millionaire.

The fact is, we can all be millionaires if we want to—we just have to work the principles God has already set in place on this planet.

The principles of compound interest show us two things.

1. **We need to recognize the importance of sacrificing early in life to start accumulating wealth.** The quicker we learn this lesson, the better off we are. The time value of money is incredibly important.

2. **The rate of our return is important.** The difference of just 1% (between 11% and 12%) becomes substantial in the long term. If we have all our savings tied up in an account at the bank that pays 2% or 3% interest, we're really just losing money every year.

THE RULE OF 72

Anybody who has ever dealt with investing money has probably heard about "The Rule Of 72." It's a math formula that we can use to calculate how long it will take for our money to double at any given rate of return.

How does it work?

We simply divide the number 72 by whatever interest rate we're getting—8%, 4%, or whatever—and the answer we come up with will tell us the number of years it will take for our money to double.

For example, if we have $10,000 getting a 10% return right now, if we divide 72 by 10, we'll find out that our $10,000 will double and become $20,000 in 7.2 years. That's not bad.

If we have stock that's appreciating in value by 5% a year, that means it will take 14.4 years to double our money. But if our stock is going up in value by 20% a year, it'll only take 3.6 years to double in value!

For those of us who started investing later in life, those higher interest rates make a big difference in how we're going to retire and what we're going to leave behind when we're gone. If we've just got a wad of cash tucked down in our sock drawer, it's never going to make anything for us.

We have to put our money where it will give us the best return possible in order to see that exponential curve start heading our way.

HOW TO HANDLE A WINDFALL

If we have recently received a large sum of money from an inheritance, an insurance settlement or something similar, what should we do to avoid ending up like those people we see on the news who win big on the lottery and then end up going broke, getting divorced and dying poor?

> *...The prosperity of fools shall destroy them.*
>
> *Proverbs 1:32*

We sure don't want our names to be put down on the list of fools, so here are three things we should do to make a financial windfall last.

1. **We shouldn't tell anybody we've got it until we talk with a CPA and a lawyer.**

   The CPA will help us with our taxes and give us recommendations about "fee-only" financial advisors who get a flat rate for their advice and don't take a percentage of what we have.

   The lawyer will help us through any legal pitfalls that may be ahead of us and be sure that our new assets are included in our estate plan.

2. **After that, we can go ahead and spend some of our money right away** to pay off our unsecured debts. If there's anything left over, it's okay to treat ourselves to a *short vacation* or to buy something *small* we've always wanted but didn't have the money for before. (**DO NOT** go out and buy that fire-engine-red Ferrari!!)

3. **We should park the rest of our money** in a money-market fund or lock it up in a CD for six months to a year. That will give us time to get a good financial education before we make any major decisions. At the end of that time, we should have gained enough knowledge about potential investments so that we can invest the rest of our windfall with confidence.

...He that believeth shall not make haste.

Isaiah 28:16

THREE PATHS TO GREAT WEALTH

1. **We need to increase our business skills.**

   It doesn't matter if we didn't take business classes in high school or college. We can go to the local bookstore or library, and get a book on business management principles. The more we learn, the more we'll increase our skills *and* our net worth.

2. **We need to increase our money management skills.**

   We're going have to learn how to manage and spend our money wisely. Maybe nobody ever taught us how to spend money wisely, but that doesn't mean we can't learn.

   To not be able to learn anything about money today, we'd have to stick our heads in the sand. There's knowledge available on finances and budgeting everywhere around us. It's on the internet, at the library, at the local community center in extension courses—and best of all—most of the information is available for free!

3. **We need to increase our investing skills.** Investments aren't just for people who are multimillionaires.

   I am not a financial counselor. I'm just a husband and a father, raising my family just like everyone else. I am not an investment expert. But I'm not ignorant, either. I've learned how to find out what I need to know.

   Even when I didn't have the money to invest in anything, I still read about investing. I also learned to ask the right questions, so when I did have money to invest, I could put it where it would bring me the best rate of return. I still read all kinds of things about where and how to invest my money so it will do the me and my family the most good.

THREE REASONS PEOPLE FAIL FINANCIALLY

Financial experts tell us that there are three major reasons people fail financially.

1. **We make wrong decisions about investments.**

   We choose low-yielding investments such as money-market funds, and CDs for our long-term investment programs, and that won't do it. The interest earned in these things rarely even beats inflation. It won't make a single dime for us. It barely maintains what we've got.

2. **We pay too much in taxes and too much for insurance (wealth leakage).**

   If we wait until the end of the year to compute our taxes, we've waited too long. We need to be able to do that on a monthly basis. Our long-term financial plans should include tax planning. We don't want to get a big refund from the government. Poor people do that. We want that money in our bank for twelve months drawing interest, not in the government's bank drawing interest.

   We also need to review our insurance coverage and needs on a regular basis—and we should never buy an insurance product as an investment.

3. **Some of us don't understand risk vs. reward.**

   There's a risk in everything we do. There's a risk in walking to the mailbox, in going to the car, and in driving to the shopping center. We can't avoid risk. We just manage it.

   Put simply, that's what investments are—they're managed financial risks we take based on knowledge. Knowing what we're doing and where we're putting our money is the key. If we totally avoid risk, we won't have any gain. (Those servants who invested the five talents and the two talents in Matthew 25 took a risk. The man who didn't want to take any risks buried his talent and God called him wicked and lazy.)

HOW TO INVEST YOUR MONEY

Now don't get all excited. I'm not going to give you any hot stock tips, or tell you how much you need to invest and what you need to invest in. I'm not even going to give you a list of ten mutual funds that you should go and sink all your money in.

Why not?

Because the individual investments that may be good for me, might not work for you in your situation.

What I am going to do is give you a list of books, publications and websites in the back of this handbook.

What you need to do is read all those books and publications and visit all those websites. Then you need to go find some more books you can read on the subject of investing—and guess what—***you're going to become a financial expert!***

The only financial expert you'll ever meet who can tell you what you need to do with your money is the one you can stare at in the mirror.

THE LANGUAGE OF INVESTING

In order to make wise decisions about how and where we're going to invest our money, we first need to learn the language financial people use.

Investments fall into five basic groups, and a good investment plan usually includes wise choices from several of these offerings.

1. **Stocks**—There are as many stocks out there as there are blades of grass in a field. There are "blue-chip" stocks for companies whose products are household words. There are stocks for medium-sized companies and small startup corporations. There are stocks from companies that work in specialized business sectors, such the banking-industry, science and technology, or bio-medical and pharmaceutical sectors. There are also thousands of international stocks. Investing in individual company stocks should be done after careful research.

2. **Mutual Funds**—Mutual funds are special managed collections of stocks based on specific sets of criteria that fit the stated goals of the funds. In other words, instead of buying single shares of one company's stock, money from multiple investors is pooled together to buy stocks from multiple companies who have something in common. There are thousands of mutual funds to choose from based on different levels of potential risk, potential growth and areas of interest. As the stocks in a mutual fund rise in value, investors share in the fund's profits. Mutual funds usually offer lower risks than many individual company stocks.

3. **Index Funds**—These are like mutual funds, except they're based on certain indices of the stock market itself, such as the S & P 500, the Dow, or the Wilshire 5000. Index funds are the favored investment of a

lot of financial experts because of their extremely low turnover and lower management expenses.

4. **Bonds**—These would include government bonds, corporate bonds and municipal bonds with terms of more than a year. A bond is basically like making a loan. Corporate bonds have averaged a total return of 6.99% and government bonds have averaged 6.51%, over the last forty years, as compared to the S & P 500 Index stocks which averaged a total of 11.18% in the same period. Financial advisors usually recommend keeping at least a small percentage of investments in bonds in order to help to balance the volatility of the stock market.

5. **Cash**—Money-market funds, U.S. Treasury Bills, short-term CDs and government bonds (with terms less than one year) fall into this category.

DIVERSIFICATION

Diversification simply means that we shouldn't put all our money in one place. There are lots of types of investments out there, so when we spread our dollars around, it helps us to minimize the risks of losing our money.

If we're in it for the long-term, even if a couple of our investments don't work out the way we planned, the money we have invested in other areas that is bringing in a good return balances out our losses. If we put everything in one place, we could lose it all overnight.

ASSET ALLOCATION

Once you start talking to financial experts, you're also going to hear the term *asset allocation.*

Asset allocation is a lot like diversification. It takes into consideration three things: our knowledge, our tolerance for risk and our need to increase our money over a certain period of time. The breakdown of how much we should invest in stocks, mutual funds, bonds, and cash, depends on how much time we have to let our money grow before we need it and on how worried we are about losing it.

A lot of experts recommend that we put 50% to 60% in stocks and/or mutual funds. Another 20% to 30% of our money might be invested in bonds backed by the federal government. (They won't make as much, but we don't have to worry about losing our shirts, since they're guaranteed.) And we could keep 10% or 15% in a money market fund or a Treasury-Bill where we could get our money quick if we needed to. (Remember we need to have at least a three-month emergency fund? That's where we keep it.)

DOLLAR-COST AVERAGING AND DRIPS

The term *dollar-cost averaging* refers to the method of putting money in an investment on a regular basis in order to take advantage of the fluctuations in its price.

Everyone knows it's a good thing to "buy low and sell high," but since nobody knows exactly when a stock price is going to rise or fall, investing a regular amount of money, even if it's only a small amount each month, buys us the most bang for our buck. Establishing a draft where a certain amount is deducted automatically from our bank account each month is the best way to make sure we get the benefit of this concept.

DRIP stands for *Dividend Re-Investment Program*. That's when we arrange to have all of our dividends and capital gains reinvested to buy more shares of a stock or a fund we own, rather than choosing to receive a check paying them to us when they are posted. DRIPs are a great way to make our money grow faster and to take advantage of dollar-cost averaging.

FIVE BIG MISTAKES INVESTORS MAKE

1. **Not having an investment plan**—Some people think they can get rich by plunking down money on a hot tip on the spur of the moment, but it isn't going to happen. The man who is diligent is the one who will prosper.

    Folly delights a man who lacks judgment, but a man of understanding keeps a straight course.

    Proverbs 15:21 NIV

2. **Buying based only on *past* performance**—Just because something did well five or ten years ago, that doesn't mean it has good growth potential over the next five or ten years. A good track record for a company or a mutual fund is definitely important, but if the company is planning a merger or the mutual fund just lost its manager, what it did in the past may not be a good indicator of how it will perform in the future. Anything we invest in should be a leader in its industry and have a bright outlook for the future.

3. **Lack of understanding**—Hosea 4:6 says that a lack of knowledge will destroy us. If we don't understand what we're investing in, we shouldn't

do it. Just because someone we heard about got rich in futures or by timing the markets, if we don't know what we're doing, we're going to loose money.

4. **Watching the markets too closely (including day-trading)**—Remember that endurance builds wealth. If we're constantly moving our money around out of fear or greed, we're digging up our seed before we can reap the harvest. We should be investing for the long-haul.

5. **Doing nothing**—If we do nothing, nothing will happen. A lot of very smart people allow themselves to become paralyzed with fear when it comes to their money. If fear of losing it is what's holding us back, we need to remember what God's Word says.

Commit to the LORD whatever you do, and your plans will succeed.
Proverbs 16:3 NIV

WORDS OF WISDOM

The great preacher John Wesley was asked one day what he thought about money.

He answered with three sentences, which when put together equal the sum-total of all financial wisdom:

Make all you can.

Save all you can.

Give all you can.

God wants us to be blessed so that we can be a blessing.

And God is able to make all grace (every favor and earthly blessing) come to you in abundance, so that you may always and under all circumstances and whatever the need be self-sufficient [possessing enough to require no aid or support and furnished in abundance for every good work and charitable donation].
II Corinthians 9:8 AMP

final
words

And Helpful
Resources

The world today is going in the opposite direction of the Church. The world's view of money is to hoard all you can so you can take care of "number one"— yourself. But God has a different idea. God's plan is for us to prosper and be in health *in direct proportion to the condition of our souls* (III John 2).

Our brains leak out information every day. That's why Romans 12:2 says that we need to renew and reload our minds—increase our souls—with the Word of God.

The more we increase our souls, the more faith we receive because we're hearing God's Word. The more faith we have, the more finances can flow through our hands to others. When our faith is working, we'll have a right attitude about money. We won't have a poverty mentality. We'll live to give, and God's abundant provision will flow to us and through us.

None of us has "arrived." Not you—and not me. The good news is that if we're not happy with where we are right now, we can always increase and grow.

We can increase in learning. We can grow in knowledge. The Bible tells us, *"Grow in grace, and in the knowledge of our Lord Jesus Christ"* (II Peter 3:18). We're not supposed to stay the same. Every day we're supposed to be further along. This year we ought to be better off than we were last year in knowledge, in material wealth and in wisdom.

So what does God want us to do?

He wants us to trust Him. We have to believe what the Bible says is true and act on it. We need to get some wisdom concerning our finances and seek the Lord about His plans for us.

> ...*They that seek the LORD shall not want any good thing.*
> *Psalm 34:10 NIV*

God doesn't want His people to be in lack. God wants us to be blessed. But He expects us to steward what we have wisely.

> *Be thou diligent to know the state of thy flocks, and look well to thy herds.*
> *Proverbs 27:23*

We have to look at our financial health and well being over the long-haul. We're not just going to read one book, quote a few scriptures and wake up the next morning with great abundance.

Learning to manage money is like training to run a long-distance marathon. People who run marathons train every day for at least a year before they're ready to go. They don't start out running thirty miles. They start out running one— then two, then five, then ten.

Getting our finances in order won't happen overnight. It takes training. It takes diligence and prayer. It takes working some Biblical principles—both Heavenly principles and principles from here on this earth. It takes some new knowledge.

Hopefully after reading this book, you have some new knowledge. Hopefully you've received some new revelation and inspiration that will help you to put the principles of God's Word to work in your finances in a new way.

As I've said before, I'm not a financial expert. I'm just a good student. I don't know everything about money, but I've learned to read and study materials written by people who are smarter than me.

I recommend that you do the same. There are some excellent materials available for you to choose from. The list I'm going to give you is just the tip of the iceberg. Some of this material comes from Christian authors, and some of it comes from the world. I don't agree with every word in every one of these books, but most of the stuff they have to say is right on target. As the old saying goes, "You can eat the hay and spit out the sticks."

My purpose in writing this book was to help you get a right perspective of what God says about money and to get your feet wet with some basic principles on how to handle finances. The rest is up to you.

I challenge you to learn one new principle or strategy for managing, budgeting or investing your finances every day for the next twelve months. Just like a marathon runner, at the end of the next year, you'll wake up to find that you're prepared to go the distance, and abundant provision will begin flowing your way.

Now get after it!

FINANCIAL MAGAZINES AND PERIODICALS

Consumer's Digest

Consumer Reports

Your Money

Kiplinger's Personal Finance

Money

SmartMoney

Business Week

Wall Street Journal

Forbes

Fortune

Worth

BOOKS ON FINANCES

Smart Couples Finish Rich
David Bach
Broadway Books

Wealth Happens One Day At A Time
Brooke M. Stephens
HarperCollins Business

The 9 Steps To Financial Freedom
Suze Orman
Three Rivers Press

Suze Orman's Financial Guidebook
Suze Orman
Three Rivers Press

The Courage To Be Rich
Suze Orman
Riverhead Books

The Financial Peace Planner
Dave Ramsey
Penguin Books

The Average Family's Guide To Financial Freedom
Bill & Mary Toohey
John Wiley and Sons

The Millionaire Mind
Thomas Stanley
Andrews McMeel Publishers

The Millionaire Next Door: The Surprising Secrets Of America's Wealth
Thomas Stanley & William Danko
Longstreet Press

The Jewish Phenomenon: Seven Keys To The Enduring Wealth Of A People
Steven Silbiger
Longstreet Press

Rich Dad Poor Dad
Robert Kiyosaki
Tech Press, Inc.

The Cash Flow Quadrant
Robert Kiyosaki
Tech Press, Inc.

Rich Kid Smart Kid
Robert Kiyosaki
Warner Books

Rich Dad's Guide To Investing
Robert Kiyosaki
Warner Books

Retire Young Retire Rich
Robert Kiyosaki
Warner Books

Flowing Wealth
David & Susie Wells
Harrison House

The Basics Of Abundance
John Avanzini
Harrison House

Wall Street Journal's Guide To Understanding Personal Finance
Kenneth Morris & Alan Siegel
Lightbulb Press

The Richest Man In Babylon
George Clason
Penguin Group

The 15 Minute Money Manager
Bob & Emilie Barnes
Harvest House

Foolproof Finances
David Mallonee
Kingdom Inc.

Money Doesn't Grow On Trees
Neale Godfrey & Carolina Edwards
Simon & Schuster

Don't Sweat The Small Stuff About Money
Richard Carlson
Hyperion Publishers

The Future Of Success
Robert Reich
Vintage Books

Multiple Streams Of Income
Robert Allen
John Wiley & Sons Publishers

Personal Finance For Dummies
Eric Tyson
IDG Books

Secrets Of The Richest Man Who Ever Lived
Mike Murdock
Honor Books

Ordinary People Extraordinary Wealth
Ric Edelman
Harper Business

I Haven't Saved A Dime, Now What?
Barbara Loos
Silver Lining Books

Master Your Money
Ron Blue
Walk Through The Bible Ministries

Money Matters For Parents
Ron & Judy Blue
Oliver Nelson Publishers

Prosperity Of The Soul
Jerry Savelle
Harrison House

Training Your Children To Handle Money
Malcolm MacGregor
Reality Ministries Inc.

The Sink Or Swim Money Program
John Whitcomb
Viking Books

The Family Manager's Everyday Survival Guide
Kathy Peel
Ballantine Books

How To Raise A Family On Less Than Two Incomes
Denise Topolnicki
Broadway Books

The 10-Day Financial Breakthrough
James Paris
River Oak Publishing

Radical Riches
Dave Williams
Decapolis Publishing

The Complete Idiot's Guide To Raising Money-Smart Kids
Barbara Weltman
Alpha Books

Family Budgets That Work
Larry Burkett
Tyndale House

Surviving The Money Jungle
Larry Burkett
Focus On The Family

Get A Grip On Your Money
Larry Burkett
Focus On The Family

Debt-Free Living
Larry Burkett
Moody Press

Your Finances In Changing Times
Larry Burkett
Moody Press

How To Invest
Nancy Dunnan
Harper Perennial

Never Balance Your Checkbook On Tuesday
Nancy Dunnan
Harper Perennial

Never Short A Stock On Wednesday
Nancy Dunnan
Harper Perennial

Taming The Paper Tiger
Barbara Hemphill
Kiplinger Times Business

A Survival Kit For Wives
Don & Renee Martin
Villard Books

The 24-Hour Turn-Around
Jim Hartness & Neil Eskelin
Revell Publishers

Secrets Of The Wealth Makers
Michael Lane
McGraw-Hill

Poor Richard's Economic Survival Manual
Alfred Munzert
Hemisphere Publications

Live Long And Profit: Wealth Building Strategies For Every Stage Of Your Life
Kay Shirley
Dearborn

Thou Shalt Prosper: Ten Commandments For Making Money
Daniel Lapin
John Wiley & Sons, Inc.

FINANCIAL WEBSITES

www.accuquote.com

www.ambest.com

www.americancentury.com

www.ameritrade.com

www.annualcreditreport.com

www.attorneyfind.com

www.bankrate.com

www.betterinvesting.org

www.careerbuilder.com

www.careerjournal.com

www.cheapskatemonthly.com

www.christianmoney.com

www.collegesavings.org

www.clarkhoward.com

www.crown.org

www.daveramsey.com

www.dca.org

www.dripcentral.com

www.ehealthinsurance.com

www.eloan.com

www.equifax.com

www.estrong.com

www.experian.com

www.fidelity.com

www.guru.com

www.hotjobs.com

www.hsh.com

www.insweb.com

www.invesco.com

www.irs.com

www.irs.gov

www.job-hunt.org

www.jobweb.com

www.kiplinger.com

www.lawinfo.com

www.lawyers.com

www.lendingtree.com

www.morningstar.com

www.moncy.com

www.moneycentral.com

www.monster.com

www.nodebtnews.com

www.nolo.com

www.prepaidlegal.com

www.quickquote.com

www.quotesusa.com

www.savingforcollege.com

www.scudder.com

www.selectquote.com

www.sharebuilder.com

www.smartmoney.com

www.ssa.gov

www.taxhelponline.com

www.taxsites.com

www.tdwaterhouse.com

www.tenday.com

www.transunion.com

www.troweprice.com

www.valueline.com

www.vanguard.com

about the author

Joe McGee

Having invested over twenty years of ministry on family, marriage and parenting issues, Joe McGee presents some of the most entertaining yet practical and insightful teaching on the family available today. This husband of thirty-plus years and father of six children is a highly sought-after special event and seminar speaker, conducting over fifty *Faith For Families Seminars* around the country each year. His sense of humor, and Bible knowledge create a wonderful laugh-and-learn experience.

Joe, his wife, Denise, and their six children
reside in Tulsa, Oklahoma.

The Vision Of Joe McGee Ministries:

Rebuilding, Reviving, Repairing And Restoring The Family

*Your sons shall rebuild the ruins of former years,
and shall revive the foundations of old, and you shall be called the
repairer of the breach, the restorer of streets in which to dwell.*
Isaiah 58:12

**Restoring Hope In Families
Through The Knowledge Of God's Word**

other resources by joe mcgee

A complete audio series of *Family Finances: Making And Managing Money* is available from Joe McGee Ministries to complement this book.

Audio/Visual Teaching Resources:

Biblical Parenting 101

Marriage Building 101

Man: Lover, Leader, Provider

Caution: Marriage In Progress

8 Things No Kid Should Leave Home Without

Leadership: Homegrown

Raising Teens

From Friendship To Courtship

Raising Happy Kids

Of Course I Love You

Family Finances: Making And Managing Money

God Knows How To Raise Your Kids: Even If You Don't

Training And Controlling Your Children

Home Free: Smoking, Drinking, and Drugs

Books By Joe McGee:

Family Finances: Making And Managing Money

God Knows How To Raise Your Kids: Even If You Don't

contact information

To contact the author, to request copy of our newsletter or our catalog of teaching materials, or to obtain information on having Joe McGee minister in your community,

Please Contact:

Joe McGee Ministries
P. O. Box 691498
Tulsa, Oklahoma 74169-1498

Or call: (918) 369-4600

Internet Address: www.joemcgeeministries.com

Please include your testimony of how this book has helped you when you write. Your prayer requests are welcome.